Prologue

My name is Michael Jean DuBois, although my sister Mia calls me "Billiard" or "Bill" for short. My sister and I are the products of Haitian parents, and Haitians believe in very strict child rearing. I guess I can remember as far back as when I was around 5 years old and my sister was 9. From that point forward, Mia and I endured about 10 years of our mother yelling at us and hitting us at the drop of a hat while our father for the most part stood idly by. Our father never hit us, but he didn't stop our mother enough from running amuck on us. He left the role of child rearing to our mother completely.

Our mother's parenting was a reign of terror, and she was harder on my sister than she was on me. Mia naturally had it tougher because her being four years older meant that she endured four more years of abuse than I did. Moreover, the degree of abuse that she got was more severe than mine. While my punishment for doing something wrong would be belt lashes or metal ruler strikes on the palms of my hands, Mom could get really perverse when she was spanking Mia. She would often have Mia take her shirt off and even drop her pants. Mia would lie on her stomach as Mom lashed her on the back and behind. And she wouldn't just hit Mia with belts or rulers. She would also hit Mia with sticks or pieces of wood. It's like sometimes Mom would look for anything she could find that would inflict the most pain. The sounds of my sister screaming with every strike are still stuck in my head today. Our mother wasn't just physically abusive, she was also verbally abusive. Mia received the brunt of the verbal assaults. Mom just seemed to look at Mia as being inadequate. She continually picked on her because she was struggling with weight. She picked on her because she had an acne problem. I was a straight A student while Mia got more B's than A's, so Mom would get on her about that.

My sister's nicknames for our mother back in the day included "Witch Hazel" and "Slave Driver." Just about every Saturday, Mia and I were obligated to clean every room of our rather large two floor house. Our mother would work on weekends; and if our cleaning wasn't done or wasn't done to her liking by the time she got home, we were lucky if she just yelled at us. There were some weekends when our mother wouldn't work and she would have plans to go to a party in the evening. On those days, it was incumbent upon us to wash her car—a snow white Toyota Corolla. Stains really stood out on that stupid white car. The lower side panels would have so many little stubborn spots, and we really had to work hard to scrub them out or else we could face our mother's wrath.

It was a very oppressive upbringing. Mom wanted to keep us cloistered from the outside world. We were only allowed to leave the house to go to school or to attend family gatherings. We were never allowed to go out with friends. In fact, there was a while when we weren't even allowed to talk with friends on the phone. When Mom would go out, she would actually disconnect the phone and take it with her so we couldn't talk on the phone. Her paranoid logic was that she didn't want any chance of us being negatively influenced by other kids.

Our father was more liberal about us hanging out with friends. Once in a while he might give us permission to go out if Mom wasn't around. However, most of the time if we needed permission to do something, he would take a pass and refer us to our mother. Our father may have been a more liberal parent than Mom, but nevertheless, he was really the lesser of two evils. He shared in our mother's philosophy about the feelings and wishes of the children not meaning a whole lot. Mia and I were living in a dictatorship. We had no say in anything. Our statements were given no credibility.

A sad example of this occurred when Mia was 12 years old and an uncle on our mother's side tried to rape her. Our parents, our mother in particular, refused to believe Mia's claim. Mom basically cross-examined her like she was a stranger on the witness stand. That uncle should have been disowned, but to this day, our mother still maintains contact with him like nothing ever happened. Try telling my sister that nothing ever happened. It's been about 30 years since the incident, and Mia is still haunted by it. She's told me that sometimes she's been traumatized by flashbacks of it over the years while she's having intimate relations with a boyfriend. In fact she had been seeing a therapist for a while in 2013.

In June of 1991, shortly after the end of my freshman year of high school, my then 19 year old sister decided that she had had enough of our mother's physical and verbal abuse. One day while our mother was at work, I watched helplessly as Mia packed up a suitcase and took a taxi to God knows where. I know she was 19, so you can't really call it a run away situation. However, I don't think Mia was quite ready to live on her own yet. It didn't matter though. She felt that she had to get out and escape the oppression. She left our New Jersey ghetto and fled to New York City where she had just completed a year of college. College was one of Mia's big bones of contention with our mother. Mia wanted to go away to the University of Miami, but Mom wouldn't allow it. She wanted Mia to continue to live at home. Therefore Mia ended up going to a school in NYC, which was close enough so that she could still live at home and commute there everyday.

Mia's sudden departure from our house had an effect on Mom that I could not foresee. Mom got much more liberal. I was never spanked again, and I was given freedom to do things and say things that I would have never been allowed before. However, the damage was done. Ten plus years of living in tyranny had molded me into a very socially awkward, timid and unconfident individual. It's a disposition that I've been struggling to overcome for the past 25 plus years, and I've just become more and more anti-social as the years have gone by. I was allowed to go away to college, and I thought that experience would make me more people friendly. It seemed like it was working for the first year and a half or so, but by my upperclassmen years I had become as anti-social as ever.

Mia came back to the house in December of 1992. She had been living with a friend from her college. Mia's return to the house was just supposed to be for a visit. Then fate intervened and she had to be hospitalized for a few weeks due to a serious flare up of a bowel disease. After she was released from the hospital, she convalesced for a little while under Mom's care and would end up moving back in the house altogether. Eventually she would settle down and get a local retail job. Unfortunately, she never got a chance to finish college.

I graduated from college in May of 1998. I didn't have a job yet so I went back home to live with Mia and the parents. In the past I had actually looked forward to coming home from college for my summer breaks, but by the time September came around, I was always pretty

4

anxious to leave. There's only so much of living with your parents that you can take. Following a very rough last semester of college in which I took on 21 credits so I could graduate on time, I went home in the summer of '98 feeling pretty worn out and lazy. I went months without even trying to look for a job. Then by New Years Day of 1999, I became galvanized by a burning desire to get my own place so I could get away from the parents.

Mia was feeling the same way. It had been about six years since Mia moved back home. She never envisioned that she'd be there that long; but as long as she was working a retail job that was paying her a pittance, she could not afford to move out. In the summer of '99, Mia graduated from a technical school where she studied to become a certified medical assistant. The salary potential was much greater than it was in retail, and by the summer of 2003 she was financially ready to move out of the house. Unfortunately however, her plans got derailed when she got fired from her job over some political bullshit. She just got into a conflict with the wrong person.

At 31 years old, I guess Mia felt she was at a crossroads. She always wanted to move to Florida, and she felt the opportunity to do it had arrived. She would start a new life and make a new living in Orlando. We had some distant cousins there who were more than happy to take her in and help her get settled, but the living arrangement would not work out. As the weeks and months went by, the family that Mia was living with became less and less hospitable. Mia would end up coming back home and rejoining me in our parents' house by the end of 2003.

In the fall of 2003, I took a big step forward in my own ambitions of moving out of our parents' house. I had gotten my first job after college in December of 2000. The pay was paltry, but I needed to get something so I could quell all my creditors. I had no chance of moving out on that salary, so I found a new job in 2003 that gave me a 23 percent increase in pay. By 2006, my performance had been rewarded with a couple of raises and bonuses. I had finally saved enough and was finally making enough to start looking for an apartment.

I really urged Mia to join me. I wanted us to get a place together. However, Mia was not in as good of a financial position as I was. After she lost her job in 2003, she ended up having to take a lower paying job that was costing her a lot of money on gas because it was about 40 miles from home. I told her that I didn't care if I had to shoulder the bulk of the living expenses as long as I could help her get away from the parents. While Mia appreciated the offer, she told me that "she did not want to live on my coattails." I could certainly understand and appreciate that. No one values independence more than I do. I had been envisioning that Mia and I would leave the house together, but I would have to leave her behind.

In May of 2007—a couple of days before my 31st birthday—I would move out of the parents' house and into my new apartment. I had been living with the parents for almost 10 years since my college graduation. For a while I was doing and feeling pretty good living on my own, but my fortunes would start to change in 2008. I was diagnosed with kidney disease early that year. I didn't feel that bad physically, accept for the fact that I had a lot of swelling from water retention in my legs. I figured out that I was taking in too much sodium. Once I cut down on the sodium in my diet, the swelling diminished dramatically. By then I had become very anti-conventional medicine, and I still am. I found an alternative medicine website that seemed to be very knowledgeable about different types of kidney diseases. I started buying supplements from that site that purportedly were specifically designed to combat my particular kidney disease. It appeared that the supplements were working, and I was feeling pretty confident that I would be okay in the long term as long as I continued to use them.

I had wanted to get away from the parents and be on my own so badly, but when I finally got what I wanted, I wasn't as happy as I should have been. It felt like something was missing. I didn't value my job as much as I should have. It felt like there was something much more interesting that I should be doing with my life. I got sick of my job. I wanted to be my own boss so I could set my own hours and not be accountable to anyone. Plus I was combating a highly anti-social disposition. I never talked to anyone at work unless I had to for business reasons. I was sick of having to be around people.

If I had valued my job more, then maybe I wouldn't have spent about two months of 2008 engaging in less than scrupulous activity that ended up getting me fired. What happened was a long, sordid and regrettable story. I really fucked myself. I made the notion of having to move back in with my parents into a potential reality.

I was too embarrassed to tell my sister and my parents about what happened, so I just told them that the office was downsized. Maybe I could have told Mia, but there was no way I was telling the parents. When you do something wrong that gets you in trouble, it would be nice if you had supportive parents to fall back on. Supportive parents may chide you a bit for what you did wrong that put you in a bad situation, but they'll encourage you and uplift you. They'll fill you with optimism that things will turn around for you.

I don't know what it's like to have parents like that. My parents are so negative, so pessimistic. When you make a mistake that gets you in trouble, my parents have a tendency to belittle you and make you feel as low and as stupid as possible. I think a big part of the reason why I'm afraid to try things and never really confide in people about my aspirations is because of fear of failure and fear of facing judgment for my failures—judgment from others and judgment from myself. I may have been programmed with those fears by my parents' negativity, and my sister can probably relate. Now granted, there was nothing really positive about what I was trying to do that led to me getting fired. I had nefarious intentions. However, in other instances when there is something positive and good to gain from trying something, fear of failure and judgment keeps you from trying—or keeps you from trying in earnest.

While I was struggling to find a new job, things were really looking up for Mia. Since I had moved out of the house, Mia had found another job that was much closer to home. Within two years she had worked her way up to a managerial position. It looked like she was on her way to being able to move out of the parents' house, and she would do just that in the fall of 2009. However, it was not the type of move that I or even she had foreseen. She was being adventurous. She was taking a leap of faith. Mia had fallen for a guy from Nebraska named Trevor who she was conversing with for several weeks on a dating website. Emails would turn into phone calls, and eventually she invited Trevor halfway across the country to the house to meet the parents. The parents seemed to like him. I got to speak with him as well, and he seemed like a good guy.

Mia had become very established and highly valued at her job, but she was willing to give it up to move to Trevor's house and start a life with him in Nebraska. It turned out to be a mistake. Within a couple of weeks after Mia's move, Trevor began to show his true colors. Mia didn't realize that Trevor was looking for a house wife. He was looking for someone to clean up after him, do his laundry and cook. She was also expected to be at his beckon call for sex, even though he had very poor hygiene. When Mia would not give Trevor what he wanted, he would get so angry that Mia was afraid he would become violent. It got to the point where she started doing whatever he wanted out of fear. Thus before the fall of 2009 was over, Mia was back home again living with the parents. She basically had to abscond from Trevor's house in the middle of the night, and then she embarked on a 20-hour, 1300 mile drive back home.

Fortunately, Mia was so loved at her previous job that they let her come back with no problem. They practically had a party to celebrate her return. Then in the summer of 2010, Mia would once again move out of the parents' house. It would take a while for her to settle down. She would move two more times over the next year. Then in the summer of 2011, Mia found a nice spacious apartment in a nice and clean building that appeared to be in a really good neighborhood. Mia had a flair for interior design, and this apartment was big enough to allow Mia to come up with a really cool and imaginative furnishing scheme.

Meanwhile, by the summer of 2011 I still had not found another job since I was let go in the fall of 2008. My unemployment benefits were exhausted, and I had no savings left. The specter of having to move back in with my parents was dancing in my mind, and I was hell-bent on avoiding that fate. I was so hell-bent on avoiding that fate that I bought a bee-bee gun and tried to rob a bank. I was arrested and spent 10 days in jail before my mother was able to come up with my bail. Eventually I would have to answer to my charges in court, but it would be several months before I got my first court date.

I was able to stay in my apartment until the end of 2011. Somehow my mother was coming up with the money to pay for my rent and utilities. I was really surprised that she agreed to do that, and I didn't ask her to do it either. She knew that I had signed a one year lease for 2011 and she didn't want me to get sued for breaking it. I was hoping I still had enough time to find a job so I wouldn't have to move back home at the end of the year, but there would be no job. I would ring in the 2012 New Year with all my furniture cramped into a small bedroom in my parents' house.

It was okay though. I was hell-bent on avoiding having to come back and I couldn't prevent it, but my mindset was that I would not be there for long. I continued to look for work with a fervor in January and February of 2012. Then all of a sudden my kidney disease took a turn for the worse. I was developing a ridiculous amount of swelling all up and down my legs, as well as in my abdomen and even in my scrotum. When the water retention seeped into my lungs and I started having trouble breathing and sleeping, I had no choice but to go to the emergency room in mid March of 2012. I received the grim news that my kidney functionality had dipped so low that I would no longer be able to survive without 12 hours a week of dialysis. I was released from the hospital after an 8 day stay and several dialysis treatments. However, I was far from free. My kidney failure had sentenced me to a lifetime of three 4-hour dialysis treatments a week. Barring a kidney transplant, my dialysis obligation ended my hopes of getting a full time job. Thus it appeared that I was doomed to having to live with my parents with no end in sight.

I remember I was watching Wrestlemania XXVIII on Sunday April 1, 2012. I vaguely remember going to my dialysis treatment the next morning, but I don't remember coming home. The next thing I remember is waking up in the hospital on Sunday April 8th. I had passed out after my dialysis treatment on Monday April 2nd and had to be rushed to the hospital. I had suffered cerebral hemorrhaging and needed emergency brain surgery. A doctor at the hospital would inform me that cerebral hemorrhaging is a risk of dialysis treatment. I spent 10 days in the hospital, although I only remember the last few days of my stay. I wasn't able to eat very much, as I would end up losing about 15 pounds. It's not like I had a whole lot of weight to spare either. I only had about 165 pounds on a 6 foot frame.

I didn't have a whole lot of time to recover from my hospitalizations before I started getting court summons regarding my attempted bank robbery charges from the previous summer. I would be in and out of court for the next four months. Because I had a clean prior record and I was a nonviolent offender, my public defender was able to convince the court to let me into the Pre-Trial Invention (PTI) program. That meant that I would be allowed to avoid prosecution and get my charges expunged from my record after completing three years of probation. My probation term included obligations of 50 hours community service, anger management counseling and a psychiatric evaluation.

Psychiatric evaluation? That's laughable. I don't think I'm crazy for trying to rob a bank when I was so desperate for money. Here's what's crazy. What's crazy is a woman having such a phobia about using public bathrooms that when she has to pee at work; she goes to a file room, squats down and pees into a jar. That's my sister for you. I'm not sure how long she had been making a habit of this, but it was long enough for someone at her clinic to catch her doing it and report her to a superior. Mia was fired in July of 2012, just a few weeks after her apartment was broken into and her laptop and ipad were stolen. That's a pretty rough summer.

My sister had made three failed attempts to move out of our parents' house and not have to come back. She had been living on her own since the summer of 2010. She was getting paid pretty well at work and had moved up in the ranks. But alas, Mia may have thrown it all away—all because she was so squeamish about using public bathrooms that she got caught peeing into a jar in a file room.

I cannot begin to convey how annoying and frustrating it is to have to live with these parents of ours. By a certain age, young men and women just are not meant to coexist with their parents in the same dwelling. Besides sharing blood, you have very little in common with people that are 30 plus years your senior. Plus in our case, we're talking about two of the most old-fashioned and non-progressive people you could think of. These people are of a time and a culture in which it was not uncommon for kids to continue living in their parents' house until they got married. I've heard stories from our mother about our grandmother spanking her full grown adult children for breaking a rule.

Like a mentioned earlier, once my sister Mia fled the house that first time in the summer of '91 when she was 19 and I was 15, Mom softened dramatically. There was no more hitting, and I was given freedom to have a social life outside of school. I felt like I had the freedom to speak my mind without fear of retribution or persecution. What has remained a problem for Mia and

I since then is the way our parents talk to us, the way they regard us and the way they look at things which is so different to the way we look at things.

No matter how old my sister and I have gotten, our parents have had a propensity over the years for treating us like little kids. In our adult years, they still lecture us when we say or do things that they don't approve of. They think that because they're the parents and they're so much older than we are, they know better about everything. As adults we've been allowed our opinions, but nevertheless; from our parents' standpoint, they are always right and we're always wrong. Trying to argue with them leads to nothing but frustration because they refuse to see or respect your side. They are extremely overbearing and unreasonable people, especially our mother.

That woman drives me nuts with how much she babies me sometimes. I was feeling fine when I came home from the hospital back in April 2012 after that brain hemorrhage. The doctors suggested that I sign up for physical therapy, but I declined it because I was having no problems with motor functions. What ensued after I left the hospital was weeks of me arguing with my mother because she kept insisting that I do physical therapy. I was fine. I didn't want it; I didn't need it. I know my body better than she does, but there was no telling her that. She just would not leave me alone, but I didn't care how much she yelled at me about it. I was not going, and I didn't go. I was already saddled with the albatross of having to go to dialysis three days a week for four hours at a time. Physical therapy would have just been another obligation, and an unnecessary one at that.

Despite our problems with the parents, Mia and I have managed to maintain a friendly rapport with them in our adult years. Well, Mia has managed to be much friendlier with the parents than I have been. When we were kids and Mom was a belt wielding tyrant, she was much more physically and verbally abusive to Mia than she was to me. So it's ironic that Mia has become particularly friendly with our mother. Nevertheless, I know that Mia will always share my resentment for this woman for the way she terrorized, cloistered and confined us when we were kids. It's a big reason why both of us have really struggled through the years with timidity, sociability, insecurity, self-worth and self-confidence issues.

As I said before, my rapport with the parents as an adult has not been as friendly as Mia's. I'll talk to Mom from time to time, but I've refrained from having intimate conversation with her. Mia is much more open with her while I am very guarded. Mia hasn't been as open with our father, but she has no problem with striking up conversation with him. As for me and our father, it has really been a non-relationship. Although Pop didn't hit us when we were kids, I grew up feeling intimidated by him. He never yelled much like our mother always did, but he always had a deep and imposing voice. Although he wasn't the tyrant that our mother was, our father still bears some of the responsibility for why my sister and I have become far from well-adjusted adults.

I've always felt nervous around that guy. Trying to talk to him has always made me feel very awkward and uncomfortable. My father is a full 43 years my senior. He has a way of making you feel stupid and unsure of yourself when you try to talk to him. With all the years he has on me, I get a sense that he feels so much wiser than I am that whatever I say is beneath him. I've felt like he has no respect for my intelligence.

It's hard to have much in common with someone who is 43 years older than you. You would think that an interest in sports is something two guys could share. However, while I've been a big sports fan since my teenage years, my father doesn't follow sports. He knows it's a subject that interests me, so from time to time he has made lame attempts to strike up conversation by asking me basic questions about a certain sport—a lot of times they're questions he's asked me already.

I've become so uncomfortable talking to him over the years that I'm even reluctant to ask him for favors. My father is a tailor. Yet there have been times when I needed little sewing jobs done on clothes, and I took the clothes to a dry cleaner that does alterations instead of asking my father to do it. For much of my adult years in my parents' house, my relationship with my father has become a perfunctory exercise of a mere daily exchange of one or two word greetings. At some point I kind of gave up on trying to talk to him, so I've had to make sure that I at least say "hi" to him once a day when I see him so he knows that I'm not angry with him for something.

There was one time back in 2002 when I was angry with him and I was withholding my "hi's" for a while. Out of the blue my father just went off on me because he didn't think he should be the only one in the house that was always taking out the trash or mowing the lawn. Those were not things I was going to volunteer to do. My standpoint was that if he wanted help with that stuff, he should've just asked me and I'd oblige him. He finished his rant on me by basically calling me a "good for nothing." His exact words were, "I was so happy I was getting a son, but all I got was a kick in the ass."

I completely ignored him after that for a couple of weeks before my mother cajoled me into forgiving him, even though he didn't exactly apologize. In fact I don't think either of them has ever apologized for any of the harsh things they've said to me or my sister. I had another issue with my father back in 2006, and it had a lot to do with him disrespecting my intelligence. Our parents are from Haiti, and they've been speaking their native language of Creole around me and Mia since we were little kids. I'm not comfortable speaking the language, but I do understand it. How could I not understand it after being exposed to it for so many years? Yet my father has assumed that because I don't speak it, I don't understand it.

So in the fall of 2006, I started noticing my father being on the phone a lot when I happened to be in the room. He would be brazenly speaking in Creole in a rather amorous and lascivious way with a woman that clearly was not my mother. One day the woman was speaking loud enough for me to make out some of her words. At one point she expressed a little worry about someone possibly being around to hear what he was saying. She said to him, "Are you sure you're alone?" He responded with, "Only my son is in the room, but he doesn't understand Creole." He chuckled as he was saying it too.

I was doubly angry with him after that. It bothered me that it sounded like he was cheating on my mother, and I was ticked off because he thought he was safe because I was too stupid to understand Creole—even though I had been exposed to it for about 25 years. So I wrote him a scathing letter and left it where I knew he would see it. I basically said that he disgusted me and that he was the stupid one for thinking that I didn't understand Creole. He exploded when he saw the letter, and a shouting match ensued between us. He was so offended that I called him stupid. How dare does someone that he considered beneath him call him stupid? I'd bet that was his standpoint.

Following that incident, I completely ignored him right through to the day I moved out of the house in May of 2007. I guess being separated from him for a while allowed our anger to dissipate, and I would be on speaking terms with him again by the end of the year.

You would think that my father would have learned his lesson about assuming that I don't understand Creole, but he showed me in 2012 that he did not. He was visiting me one day when I was in the hospital for kidney failure. He was sitting in the corner talking on his cell phone, and I'm listening to him as he starts making snide and derisive comments about me in Creole. Somehow it was beyond him to understand why I wanted to go home so much. He was saying to his phone partner, "What does he want to go home so much for? What's he gonna do there?" I wanted to interrupt him and say, "Hey, I know you're talking about me. I understand everything you're saying. Leave me alone. Get the fuck out of here!" However, I kept my sentiments to myself and let his disrespect go.

I had been living on my own for about 5 years before I had to move back in with my parents in January of 2012. I didn't have to be back in the house for very long to realize that I had forgotten just how annoying my parents were to be around every day. I had really enjoyed the peace and quiet that came with living by myself. That was over when I was back in the house, as my parents are two obnoxiously loud people. My mother has always been a very irritable hothead. She's always complaining and yelling about something. She loves to talk; and even if she's not yelling, she still has an obnoxiously loud speaking voice. We live in a rather large two floor house—three if you count the basement. No matter where this woman is speaking in the house, her voice fills the entire the house. She loves talking on the phone, and she makes her phone calls doubly noisy by walking around with the speaker phone on for no apparent reason. So I'm forced to become privy to both sides of one of her conservations when I don't want to be.

My father is obnoxiously loud, but in a different way than my mother. By 2012, my father is 79 years old and has been retired for a number of years—other than a small job in the morning delivering newspapers, which he would also retire from by the end of 2013. He's always home, and he seems to have this habit of going up and down the stairs for what seems like every 10 minutes. It's annoying because he has very loud and heavy footsteps. If he's not on his cell phone or taking a nap, which he does about two to three times a day, he just seems to be wondering aimlessly about the house. It's almost impossible for this guy to move from one area of the house to another without being musical. He's constantly singing, or humming, or whistling. You can be in a room by yourself, and it's nice and quiet. Then this guy will come in the room and start making noise with loud singing, humming or whistling. He's totally unabashed and completely inconsiderate of others. He's going to do what he does, and you just have to grin and bear it.

Besides my parents being obnoxiously loud, what also annoys me about my parents is that they're religious fanatics while I have been an atheist since 2009. My father is a bible-thumping conservative. He takes everything in that book literally. He is so anti-gay. He once opined to me that God should punish homosexuals when they have sex by making them get pregnant and give birth to monkeys. My mother may be a little more liberal about homosexuality. She's always been a very devout Catholic, but when I came back to the house in 2012, I realized that she had become almost insanely religious. It's thanks in large part to a Catholic worship channel that she found on our cable system. It's her favorite channel. At least half the time she spends watching TV everyday is dedicated to that channel.

My mother has always gone to church every Sunday. That's what you're supposed to do as a Catholic. However, in addition to every Sunday, she also goes to church every Wednesday night at midnight. This woman is in her 60s and has a very physically taxing job at a nursing home where she works a 3pm to 11pm shift, then has to endure a 45 minute drive home. Yet every Wednesday night you know she's going to be home later than usual because she has to go to church for an hour before coming home. So she goes to church every Sunday morning, every Wednesday night, and she watches a mass every morning on that Catholic channel. She's constantly praying and talking about praying. She'll try to preach to me about God and prayer even though I told her I'm an atheist. I do the best I can to put up with it without saying something to disrespect her beliefs, even though she doesn't have a problem with disrespecting mine.

When my sister Mia told me in July of 2012 that she lost her job, the first thing I thought of was the possibility of her having to join me in our parents' house. While I thought it would be nice to have someone to commiserate with, I was rooting very hard for her to find a way to avoid that fate. By the summer of 2012 I had saved enough money from my disability benefits to be able to purchase an iphone. I finally got rid of my old flip phone that I had purchased back in 2005. Texting was so cumbersome with that phone. It would take me like 5 minutes to write one little sentence. With the iphone, I was able to start texting rapid fire. I would start texting Mia fairly regularly. Mia's really the only person I text. She's just about the only friend I've had since college.

My first text to Mia with my iphone was on August 21, 2012. By then Mia had already gotten another job, but she made the tough decision of settling for one that paid substantially less than she was making before. She didn't want to wait for something better to come along and end up not getting anything at all. She would be doing okay for a little while, but eventually her expenses would start overwhelming her.

What follows now is record of the text exchanges between me and Mia from August 21, 2012 to the date of May 1st, 2014. The significance of May 1st 2014 is that it would be the first day of our mother's retirement. Mom's annoying to be around everyday, but at least there was a break from the annoyance when she went to work. Starting on May 1st 2014 it would be the new reality of getting used to her being home just about all day and everyday. Back in August of 2012, Mom was still working full time and doing double shifts just a few months after her 65th birthday. Her retirement was on hold but none of us—including her—was sure of how long it would be on hold. At this point she had been unsuccessfully trying to sell the house for the past few years. Her plan was to use the proceeds from the sale to get a condo in Florida with our father.

On August 21st 2012 I was starting my first day of community service as part of my Pre-trial Invention probation obligation from my attempted bank robbery in 2011. Luckily I had just bought my iphone, otherwise I would have been really bored. There really wasn't much for me to do. I was kind of just serving time about two to three times a week for about 4 hours at a time until my 50 hour obligation was met. I sent my first iphone text to Mia at 1:01pm.

Tuesday August 21, 2012, 1:01pm

Me: Messing around with new iPhone 4s

Me: Starting 50 hrs comm serv at a library for my court case. Just sitting on comfy chair. Nothing to do yet.

Mia told me later on that she didn't respond to my texts because she had no idea who was texting her. A new cell phone number came with my new cell phone, and she didn't recognize the number.

Wednesday August 22, 2012, 8:52pm

Me: Can u get day off on 9/18?

Wednesday August 22, 2012, 10:18pm

Mia: What's on 9/18?

Me: Transplant evaluation

Mia: Where?

Me: Either University or Beth Israel hospital

Mia: Not sure yet. Just got perm position at work. Can't really take days off yet. If I do, I won't get paid for that day. But I'll see.

Me: Ok

Mia lost her job a few months earlier, but it did not take her long to find a temp job that turned into a permanent position, although she had to settle for markedly less pay than her previous job. By the way, you would not believe what she did to lose her previous job. My sister has a serious phobia about using public bathrooms. She has such a phobia, that she would go into a file room and pee into a plastic container because she was so leery about sitting on a public toilet. Unbeknownst to her, someone caught her peeing in the file room and reported it to her manager. She was fired shortly thereafter.

Mia: So glad u got an iphone. How are u liking it?

Me: I got an app that lets me listen to my sports radio show on my phone! It's tremendous

Mia: Isn't it? It's a beautiful thing. What app is it?

Me: CBS local radio road show

Mia: Nice. There's another cool app that I have on my iphone and tablet called Tunein radio. It's awesome. Tons of radio stations by genre, even sports radio. I even saw WFAN. Did u download iTunes in your computer yet?

Me: Not yet. If I connect the phone to USB, will the computer give download instructions?

Mia: No. I forget how I did it. I think you need to go to Apple's website. You should do the download so you'll always be able to back up your iphone.

Me: I'm lookin into it.

Mia: The download takes a while. I think it's about 45 min. Make sure you can spare your computer for at least that long

Me: The apple site isn't letting me download, but I think I'm able to backup thru iCloud if I'm connected to wi-do.

Me: Wi-do

Mia: Ok

Me: Trying to say wi-go

Me: U know what I mean. The auto correct is kind of nice, but it's killing me here.

Thursday August 23, 2012, 1:11 am

Mia: To download iTunes on your computer, go to iTunes.com/download

Me: Gotcha.

Thursday August 23, 2012, 1:29pm

Me: B some scary shit if these republicans take the white house. They'd outlaw abortions no matter what the circumstances, they're anti birth control. They're basically anti out of wedlock sex not resulting in a baby.

Me: Silver lining I guess is that even with a republican president, he can't do what he wants if congress is mostly democrats.

Mia may not have responded because she's just not into politics. I wasn't very political myself until around 2008. I think the campaign and the election of our first black president aroused me to start following politics.

Sunday August 26, 2012, 1:27pm

Me: What is it about this "call me maybe" song that has caused such hysteria? Are u into it too?

"Call Me Maybe" by Carly Rae Jepsen. A song played so much in the summer of 2012 that it got really annoying.

Mia: I'm pretty familiar with it, and it is getting pretty annoying.

Monday August 27, 2012, 9:14pm

Me: Can't believe I just watched a Haitian on tv playing professional tennis.

Mia: Word?! What's the name?

Monday August 27, 2012, 10:52pm

Me: Victoria Duval, only 16 yrs old

I was watching one of the biggest tournaments in professional tennis, The US Open. Mia's not a sports fan, but I figured she'd be interested about this given that we're Haitian.

Thursday August 30, 2012, 12:50pm

Me: Very tough question. U don't have to answer right now, u can just tell me you'll think about it. If u were a match, would u be willing to give me a kidney?

Thursday August 30, 2012, 1:57pm

Mia: I've already thought about it. I figured that's why you asked me to come to the transplant evaluation with you. It is a tough question. If I was healthy, I would give you one in a heartbeat. We're also talking about major surgery, which would involve a period of recovery. Who would support me while I'm not working?

Me: I understand, but see if u can come with me on 9/18 anyway for more info

Mia: Ok

I figured that if I had any hope of working full time again so I could eventually move out of my parents' house, I would have to get a kidney transplant so I wouldn't need dialysis anymore. The waiting list for a transplant is years long, so you really hit a jackpot if you're able to find a

relative willing to give you a kidney. And Mia is really the only relative that I'm close with.

Friday August 31, 2012, 9:11pm

Me: Can't wait for your mom to go back to work!

Mia: What did she do?

Me: As you know, Aunt Anita is also dealing with kidney failure/dialysis. Aunt Anita's protein levels are low, so that makes Mom concerned about my levels. So she talks about me eating more meats than just chicken and fish. I told her that I know my levels are fine so I'm not changing my diet. I had to say this repeatedly as she kept trying to convince me to eat other meats. I told her she was making my blood pressure go up by not listening to me. Then she basically says I'm wrong for getting upset. At the core it's still the same woman we loathed as kids. She can never be wrong about anything.

Mia: I'm not going to take sides on this one. But what I can say is this, in life you have to pick your battles. Mom has come a long way from being that woman that raised us with an iron fist. However, she still has the same basic need to control everyone and everything around her. And she always has to be right, which is also her way of trying to maintain control. Unfortunately, she has also become increasingly more difficult to reason with at times. The control instinct kicks in when she's scared or worried. You almost died. So she's just concerned. Cut her some slack. Just tell her that you understand where she's coming from, but it overwhelms you at times

I think Mia saying that I almost died is a hyperbolic statement. Maybe she was thinking of the brain hemorrhage I suffered in April of 2012, but that was not a result of my kidney condition. It was kind of a side effect of dialysis. I feel like Mia apologizes for Mom too much. When we were kids, Mia basically wished this woman dead everyday. I just don't understand why and how Mia has come to befriend this woman so much. After the summer of 2010 when Mia moved out of our parents' house and I was still living on my own, Mia would visit the parents 2 or 3 times a month and would actually spend entire weekends at the house.

Me: Never felt so trapped in my life. I need a transplant. Cause as long as I'm on dialysis I can't work, which means I can never leave this house.

Mia: That's pressure

Me: Did not mean to press. Hey it's only pressure if you are a match. The president gives a state of the union address. I'm just giving u the state of the billiard.

"Billiard" is a nickname that my sister started using to address me many years ago. Don't know how she came up with it, but it has stuck ever since. Sometimes she just addresses me as "Bill" for short.

Me: U familiar with Anderson Cooper? He hosts a political show weeknights on CNN. He revealed this past week that he was gay.

Mia: Yes. Had a crush on him briefly after the Haiti earthquake. And questions regarding his sexual orientation had been buzzing around the rumor mill for quite some time. So it's really no surprise

Me: Is there anybody left who isn't gay? Who knows how many are, but are reluctant to come out.

Mia: I know. It seems to be the trend these days.

Me: Anybody that u suspect is gay?

Mia: I've heard Queen Latifah may be a lesbian. That rumor has been around for a while and it def wouldn't surprise me if it was true. She's always been a little "butchy" and I've never seen her with a man or speak of any particular male love interest. But then again, she may be just a very private person. I also heard that Robin Roberts, one of the co-hosts on GMA is a lesbian

Me: Remember Queen Latifah was gay in Set it Off.

Mia: Yep. I was thinking about that as I was texting you about her. Maybe that was art imitating life

Me: The gay couple on Modern Family. The bearded guy is gay in real life.

Mia: I know. I saw him on Ellen a while back. So is David Hyde Pierce who played Kelsey Grammer's brother on Frasier, and Ricky Martin finally came out recently

Me: Pierce did come off kind of feminine. Wonder if Will from Will and Grace is real life gay. Could half the population be gay? Wonder what the percentage is, keeping in mind how many people may not want to come out.

Mia: That's a good question. But I think it just seems like gays are fast becoming the majority. Since they have more freedom and are being granted the same rights as heterosexuals, they are coming out of the closet

Me: Did u see the picture I sent you of my old roommate from July of 1993 and his hot little wife? Boy did he get fat. Do you remember him? He's the kid who showed me how to play Spit.

Mia: I remember him. He was this skinny geeky looking kid with blonde hair and glasses. His wife looks like he met her at a strip club.

Me: U remembered him well. When I found his profile on facebook, I was just really struck by how fat he got and how his wife is as hot as he is fat.

Mia: Lol. She also looks younger than he is

Me: I think she's Russian. Gotta love those Russian accents. Sultry and sophisticated.

Monday September 17, 2012, 10:18pm

Me: What's up with mom's work schedule? She's only worked one day since last Tuesday.

Tuesday September 18, 2012, 12:05am

Mia: Mom gets these random days off called holidays. Anyway, I got the day off. Do you still want me to go with you to the transplant evaluation?

Me: Yes. Be at the house by 10:30am and we'll go to the hospital from there. Thanks.

Tuesday September 18, 2012, 5:21pm

Me: If u feel bad about the donor thing, u don't have to. They probably wouldn't let u because they're looking for people in the best health.

Mia's afflicted with ulcerative colitis.

Mia: I do feel bad. You have no idea how much I want you to resume the quality of life that you had and how much I would love to be the one to help you get it back

Me: Don't worry about it. The donor should be in good health not just for the sake of the recipient, but also for their own sake so they won't have issues recovering from a major surgery.

Me: 2 hr special at 9 tonight on ABC ranking the top tv shows of all time.

Mia: Oh ok..Should be interesting

Tuesday September 18, 2012, 9:14pm

Me: No Friends in top 5 sitcoms of all time? What the fuck?

Mia: What????

Mia: I'm not watching the show presently. Which ones made the top 5? I bet MASH was one of them

20

Me: You're right. Mash, All in the Family, Cosby Show, Seinfeld and I Love Lucy. That's the order from #5 to #1.

Mia: I knew All in the Family would have been among the list and I figured probably the Cosby Show. Totally forgot about I Love Lucy (how could I forget that one), but Seinfeld? That one kind of shocks me. It was a funny show yes, but it doesn't get my vote as one of the top 5

Me: No Friends on that list? How is that possible?

I was pretty shocked to find that Mia doesn't regard Seinfeld as highly as I do. It doesn't seem like she's as high on Friends as I thought either.

Me: Saw a portion of a George Clooney interview from 1995. He was looking and sounding like the big brother of Pacy from Dawson's Creek.

Mia: Yeah I always thought there was a resemblance between those 2. Whatever happened to that kid anyway? He just fell off the face of the planet

Me: Joshua Jackson actually has been on a show called Fringe since 2008 on Fox 5.

Mia: Oh? What's that show about?

Me: It looks kind of like the X-Files

Me: It's on Friday nights so it's probably not one of fox's big money makers. The only worse night for a show to get a good audience is Saturday.

Mia: Watching CSI: Miami on WE. Can't believe Eva LaRue is 46

Mia: And she def doesn't look like she's had any work done

Mia: Why are Friday & Saturday nights bad nights for TV shows to air on?

Me: It's the weekend. People go out on Friday nights and especially go out on Saturday nights. Thursday night lineups have always been a big deal I guess because it's like the last night of the tv week in terms of big viewership.

Mia: Ok, that was pretty much my theory. Wasn't sure if it was accurate. I guess they didn't have very high hopes for a series that I liked called Common Law. It aired on Friday nights on USA

Me: U always have to be worried about the future of one of your shows if it gets moved to Friday night or especially Saturday night. It's like the show is moved to death row. Is that show still airing?

Mia: No. I think it's on hiatus right now. But they're not even airing repeats. I wonder if it's coming back for another season

Me: U could probably find out if u google it.

Friday September 21, 2012, 8:18pm

Me: Google lady gaga if u haven't seen most recent pics of her. She's put on 25 lbs! Sad sight.

Mia: Yeah I saw her on the E Channel. Pretty stunning.

Saturday September 22, 2012, 9:22pm

Me: Just heard the loudest thunder clap ever. It was like an explosion.

Mia: It was pretty loud here too

Mia: Did you know you could send voice text with your iPhone?

Me: Did not know that.

Mia: Just press the little microphone key to the left of the space bar

Me: Don't see that key on the keypad.

Mia: It's to the left of the space bar

Me: There's no mike key to the left of the space bar on this keypad.

Mia: Guess maybe my iPhone version is a little different than yours.

Thursday September 27, 2012, 12:40pm

Me: What's your top 5 favorite tv comedies you've ever seen? Hard to narrow it down. Here's mine: Friends, Seinfeld, Married With Children, Three's Company, Honeymooners. Honorable mention to Ally McBeal, technically a dramedy, but it gave me a lot of gut-busting laughs.

Mia: Yeah, this is a hard one to narrow down. I Love Lucy, All in the Family, The Golden Girls, Threes Co (but only until Chrissy gets stupid), The Jeffersons (first few seasons)

I'm shocked that we only have one show in common for our top 5's. Again, I'm really surprised that she doesn't have Friends or Seinfeld; and she has a couple of shows on her list—The Jeffersons and All in The Family—that you couldn't pay me to watch.

Thursday September 27, 2012, 6:41pm

Mia: Hey billiard. Would you happen to have any surplus of food stamp money left? I feel like shit for asking, but the worst you can say is no

Me: How much do u need? Tough time to ask. Only have $53 left and don't get replenished until next week.

Thursday September 27, 2012, 11:24pm

Mia: I guess I know what the answer is. Don't worry about it. I'll manage somehow

Mia's really starting to struggle financially at this point. A couple of months with a job paying her much less than her previous one is starting to catch up to her now.

Wednesday October 3, 2012, 4:25pm

Me: Must see tv tonight at 9. Presidential debate #1. If u watch tonight, watch channel 4.

I know Mia's not politically inclined, so I should've been surprised that I didn't get a response here. But sometimes you're so pumped up about something that you want somebody to share in your excitement.

Thursday October 4, 2012, 8:04pm

Me: Was watching a documentary about all these retired athletes that blew millions of dollars thru reckless spending and ended up bankrupt. One of the problems is that these guys can't keep their pants zipped. They end up fathering several children with different women and owe like 50 gees a month in child support. Apparently Evander Holyfield has like 13 kids with 9 different women!

Mia: Dang!

Me: My mistake. Just confirmed on Wikipedia. Evander Holyfield actually has ONLY 11 kids with 6 different women.

Sunday October 7, 2012, 2:57pm

Me: Never know what you're gonna see on antenna tv channel 252. Shows tonight include WKRP in Cincinnati, Barney Miller and Benson. Still waiting for some channel to bring back What's Happening.

Mia: Benson! Been a while since I've seen that show. And yeah, still waiting for that one too. You would think that Centric or TV One or BET would air it.

Me: U wonder if What's Happening may have been banished because it kind of made light of spanking. Just a theory. Not a fan of that aspect, but would love to see the show again nevertheless.

Wednesday October 10, 2012, 7:34pm

Mia: Threes Co is on Antenna TV right now. It's the "God forgot to wind it" episode

Me: Watching now.

Me: Larry gets Jack into so much trouble. Larry should be the one Max wants to kill.

Mia: I agree. I know that's how the show had to play out, but Larry sucked as a friend. He's the Eddie Haskell to Jack's Wally

Me: Right. PS, look at Cindy's top. Boy she was hot.

Me: Mr Furley fainting in the background. Funny!

Mia: Yeah! That must have hurt

Me: Would love to see some outtakes. Jennilee Harrison must have had a tough time delivering the "God forgot to wind it" line with such a straight serious face.

Sunday October 14, 2012, 10:03pm

Mia: I think I might have to join you and move back in with the parents.

Me: What happened?

Mia: First of all I got a letter that I have to appear in court on Oct 30 because my Sept rent hadn't been paid. I did pay it but it was late. Since I'm making less money, paying my rent has been a struggle. It's really fucked up in light of the fact that I was robbed in my own building about 4 months ago and they still haven't replaced my broken door

I thought that Mia was living in a good neighborhood. That robbery really shocked me. I think it might have been an inside job. It could have been perpetrated by someone living in her building.

Me: This is the exact opposite of lol. It's col.

Mia: Opposite?

Me: Not a funny situation so it makes u wanna col. Cry Out Loud.

Mia: Trust me. I feel like I'm on the verge of tears

Me: U at home now?

Mia: No I'm at work

Me: Temp is relatively pleasant despite the overcast. Was going to suggest u put your sneaks on and take a walk.

Mia: If I was home I'd go running

Me: U able to make a viable excuse to leave work now?

Mia: No and I haven't earned enough time off so I can't afford to leave early

Me: Hang in there, sweetie puss.

Mia: Trying. Just feel like I keep getting blind sided

Me: I know snookums. Gotta get to the end of the tunnel and meet that light.

Mia: Yeah. I've just gotta try to stay positive.

Monday October 15, 2012, 6:57pm

Me: If u had an extra $150-$200 a month, would that be enough to make ends meet? If so, then it might be worth it to apply for food stamps. But if approved, u wouldn't start getting anything til about 2 months after u started the application process. But at least the benefits would be retroactive to the start date of your application. If u applied in October and start getting benefits in December, the amount u got in December would include amounts for October and November.

Mia: Can I apply online?

Me: That would be great, but unfortunately u have to apply in person. And u have to be prepared to wait a while because they're so many applicants. The first time I went, I got in line and when I got to the window, they took some basic info and gave me and appointment letter to come back in a month.

Mia: Ok

Me: It's a frustrating, annoying app process, but it is worth going thru if it would really help u. You'd probably have to take a day off it you go down there because of the potential wait time. Let me know if/when u decide to go.

Mia: Ok. I'm imaging what the place looks like

Me: It's not that bad, except that you'll be surrounded by a lot of ghetto type people. The office opens at 7:30am I believe. Or 8:00am, don't remember exactly. U wanna get there when it opens to reduce wait time. Problem is that others are thinking the same thing. Sometimes they don't open the doors right away so when u get there u may see a line wrapped around the building of people waiting to be let in. Be prepared when u get in to have to go thru metal detectors, and u may be asked to empty your pockets, take off your coat and take off your belt if you have one on. Don't be turned off. If u need it u have to go for it. Maybe you'll meet my case worker friend—the one I refer to as "Twelve Tooth" because she has so many teeth missing. Keep in mind that you'll have to pay for parking. There's a parking lot across the street from the building. I think they charge $3 an hour.

Mia: I think if I go, I'll take the bus. I hate taking the bus, but it would be cheaper than paying for parking.

Me: Bussing it is what I did later on. But sometimes you're just not in the mood to wait for a bus. From where you live, you may actually have to take two busses. Go to njtransit.com to confirm. U put in your starting point and destination and they'll tell u exactly what to do.

Mia: Ok. Thanks Bill. This was all really helpful

Me: Good luck. If it would really help u, then u have to go for it.

Saturday October 20, 2012, 6:25pm

Me: What's wrong with your mom? She's got into this habit of talking to people on speaker phone. Doesn't she know that's impolite?

Mia: Yeah, I hate that. Patients do that all the time when I'm on the phone with them at work

Me: Maybe she just discovered the phone's speaker capability, and it's like a toy she likes playing with. I hate it because I gotta hear two loud Haitian voices instead of just one.

Friday October 26, 2012, 4:44pm

Me: Just saw 46 yr old Halle Berry on Ellen. Forgot how hot she is cause I don't see her that often. Shame on me. She's the ultimate chocolate milf.

Mia: Lol. She's in some new movie

Me: Looks good. It's called Atlas. It's about reincarnation. Apparently her character gets reincarnated several times over a 500 yr span.

Friday October 26, 2012, 7:45pm

Mia: I heard a review about Atlas on the radio this morning. Unfortunately it wasn't a good one

Me: Still would be interested in checking it out for the sheer spectacle of it. Reminds me of Inception, a movie a couple of years ago about the dream world. A little hard to follow, but a fascinating watch.

Sunday October 28, 2012, 3:16pm

Mia: Are u still at dialysis?

Me: Yes

Mia: Ok. I thought you were home. I wanted to know if mom was home and I don't feel like calling the house

Me: Didn't work yesterday so I assume she is home

Mia: Ok

The dialysis clinic was expecting to have to close for a day due to the impending Hurricane Sandy, therefore my dialysis schedule for the week was changed to Sunday, Wednesday Friday.

Monday October 29, 2012, 10:50pm

Mia: Did you guys lose power?

Me: No. Did you?

Mia: No. The lights just flicker every now and then when the wind blows.

Me: Trying to stay calm despite these ridiculous wind gusts. Never heard anything like this.

Mia: I know They said this is the worst to hit this area in a number of years. Every time that wind blows, I panic. There are a lot of trees around here and the parking lot is surrounded by a bunch of them

Me: Global warming/climate change. The Northeast never had to deal with hurricane winds. Now we got this two years straight. Hope we're long gone before this weather gets any worse.

Me: People that study the weather think that if the patterns continue, by year 2200 we could have hurricanes that would leave NYC completely underwater.

We live in the Northeast, and the Northeast was really hit hard by Hurricane Sandy. Our particular area was actually spared compared to the damage done to counties within 50 miles of us. Still our area had a lot of downed trees and power lines. The wind was so strong that night that I was afraid it was going to break the windows. Hurricanes are not supposed to hit the Northeast, especially nothing as strong as Sandy. Global warming/climate change is real.

Tuesday October 30, 2012, 6:25pm

Me: Long Island and Staten Island look like New Orleans after Katrina. So does South Jersey.

Mia: I couldn't get to work. I drove around for nearly an hour and could not access the main road

Me: Trees right?

Mia: Trees, power lines, police tape, some streets were barricaded by cop cars or fire engines. What I saw as drove just made my jaw drop

Me: NYC subway system is shut down. The tubes that run under water are flooded. One good thing about that flooding. Maybe it will flush out the rats.

Mia: Lol

Wednesday October 31, 2012, 6:45pm

Me: Imagine living in parts of Newark right now that don't have power.

Mia: I heard that there's looting going on in a lot of areas without power.

Wednesday October 31, 2012, 10:36pm

Me: No surprise. Imagine how spooked you would be from any little noise u hear when you're in the dark. Btw, it's clock setback time on Sunday. Even more darkness. They should postpone that so there's more daylight time for cleanup efforts, and less darkness for communities without power.

Mia: Makes sense. I wonder if Chris Christie and President Obama thought about that today during their aftermath of Sandy meeting

Me: Wish they did.

Me: Back in 2010 with the Haiti earthquake, u were being bombarded with so many disaster images on the news. A comedian characterized it as disaster porn. It's gonna get to that point with the Sandy aftermath. There's even a post 9/11 feel to it. Regular programming has not been on NBC since Monday.

The comedian I was referring to is Bill Maher. I started watching his comedic political show on HBO back in 2008. Bill Maher is a proud atheist who enjoys disparaging religion. He gets all the credit for my conversion to atheism. Thanks Bill!

Thursday November 1, 2012, 6:55pm

Me: How bout the visual of Obama next to Chris Christie. The number 10 comes to mind. He looks like twice Obama's width. If Obama is a 34 waist, Christie is at least a 60.

Mia: At least.

Saturday November 3, 2012, 5:42pm

Me: I drove by a line of people waiting to get gas that was about 3 blocks long.

Mia: Was it for Sunoco?

Me: Yeah I think it was.

Mia: Fuck. That's usually where I get gas.

Saturday November 3, 2012, 7:10pm

Me: U running low? I get the idea that we're about a week from normalcy. Apparently if u look under #njgas on twitter, u can find open gas stations in nj. Looks like top half of nj is on short supply, bottom half is at close to normal supply.

There was a tremendous gas shortage going on in New Jersey for about 2 to 3 weeks after Hurricane Sandy.

Tuesday November 20, 2012, 9:26pm

Me: Thanksgiving on ch. 11 at 9am. March of the Wooden Soldiers followed by 6 hrs of The Honeymooners.

Mia: Word?! Sweet

Thursday November 22, 2012, 6:28pm

Mia: Benson on Antenna TV on Sunday nights

Me: Cool.

Friday November 23, 2012, 8:23pm

Me: Major milestone last night. Got to 500,000 point mark in marathon Tetris for first time. 510,965 to be exact. Game lasted 33 minutes and ended on level 14.

Mia: Damn

Tuesday December 4, 2012, 6:26pm

Me: Reunited, and it feels so good...Turns out the hospital has a safe they keep valuables in that patients come in with. Anything you had on u that goes in the safe is listed on a separate sheet of paper from everything else u came in with. Stumbled onto that separate valuables sheet last night.

Mia: Ohhhhh GOOD! I'm so glad. I felt so bad when you thought that you lost your iPhone. There are still honest people in this world.

Me: Had the pleasure of getting stitches in my head after the tube was taken out yesterday. Not sure what was worse to deal with—the pain while I was getting the stitches or the pain after the stitch job was done.

Mia: Ooooh. My heart just ached

Back in late November to early December of 2012, I was hospitalized one more time for another brain hemorrhage. It may have been precipitated by a very high blood pressure I had when I left dialysis the day before. The last reading I remember was a staggering 247 over 142. Thankfully as of May 2014, I have not had another brain hemorrhage since. After the surgery, they left a tube in my head with a little plastic container attached. I was supposed to sleep on my side so the excess fluid in my skull could drain out through the tube and collect into the container. After a few days, they had to pull the tube out and stitch up the hole. Youch!!

The second brain hemorrhage was less severe than the first one. When I came home after the first one in April of 2012, it actually took me about a week to remember how to type and to remember my internet passwords. I also remember not recognizing the house when I came home. I didn't have any memory issues after the second brain hemorrhage. However, I felt like there were times when I was in a really altered reality when I was in the hospital. I remember feeling like my bed was moving from one area of my room to another. I was actually feeling like I was the one that had a special power to make my bed move. I would just close my eyes and focus on the bed moving, and when I would open my eyes, me and my bed were in a different area of the room.

Thankfully, this hospital stay didn't cost me my iphone. I had no memory at all of being admitted into the hospital, so I had no idea of where it was.

Friday December 14, 2012, 7:26pm

Me: I'm numb to these shootings. After the mass shooting in Aurora, I emailed every single congressman (over 500 of them) about the need for enhanced gun control. Wasted keystrokes. Wasted breath. The person who did this should be sentenced to an eternity of being burned to death, revived, then burned to death again.

Mia: Dang Billiard, don't hold back. Tell me how you really feel.

Mia: But I do agree

I was lamenting about the Newton, CT school shooting in which 20 first graders were killed. When I had heard about the mass shooting at a movie theater in Aurora, CO in the summer of 2012, I was so ticked off over that one that I spent about a week emailing every congressman. No surprise that I didn't change a thing. All these congressman are beholden to and scared of the NRA. Or they hide behind the 2nd Amendment's decree of "the right to bear arms." Notwithstanding the fact that the 2nd Amendment is so outdated and obsolete because it was put in at a time when we were a very young country that was afraid of the British trying to overtake us again.

Monday December 17, 2012, 5:30pm

Mia: You have such a way with words. Here's a suggestion...W-R-I-T-E

Monday December 17, 2012, 8:43pm

Me: I do indeed have writing plans for 2013.

Mia: You do?!

Me: Yes

Mia: That's awesome. It's also one of my goals for the new year

I was true to my word. In January of 2013 I would start working on my life story. I actually had started it a couple of years earlier, but I only managed a couple of paragraphs. I was a little distracted because I was so focused on trying to find a job so I could avoid having to move back in with the parents. In January of 2013, I would start writing my story in earnest.

Tuesday December 25, 2012, 1:24pm

Me: How do u lose sheep?

Mia: ?

Me: I was talking about March of the Wooden Soldiers. It's on right now.

Mia: Yeah I just noticed as I was channel surfing

Tuesday December 25, 2012, 7:38pm

Me: Don't remember this as part of the Christmas decorations last year. Standing up in front of the fireplace right now is this gnome-sized Santa Claus. It's actually a tad creepy.

Mia: Is he made of felt with gold wire-rimmed glasses?

Me: Think so. Don't remember if it has glasses.

Mia: It does. And it looks especially creepy in shadow if you happen to be going downstairs in the dark

Me: I first saw it when I was going downstairs the other night with the lights off and that Santa was illuminated by the fireplace light. I was like, what the fuck is that?

Wednesday December 26, 2012, 2:45pm

Mia: Is it snowing out and how bad is it?

Me: I'm at dialysis, can't get up to look out the window

Mia had texted me from work. She was worried about the snow for her drive home. This was our last text exchange until February 2, 2013. In the interim, Mia's financial situation forced her to move back into the house with me and our parents in January of 2013. She's all cramped up in the little bedroom adjacent to mine, which actually used to be my bedroom before I had moved out in 2007. I thought getting food stamps could've helped her avoid having to come back to the house, but it looks like she never looked into it for some reason.

In December of 2012, I received some devastating news. I was told by one of the doctors conducting my kidney transplant evaluation that my particular kidney disease was so devilish that if I got a transplant, my body would most likely reject it within a few months. A kidney transplant was a great chance for me to get my old life back. Now that was not going to happen. So I started planning my suicide. I had enough money in my bank account to use to buy a gun. February 2, 2013 was on a Saturday. On that Saturday morning, I had made plans to take a train to Pennsylvania where a gun show was going on that day. However, before I purchased the train ticket, I got really scared about the possibility of having my bag checked when I would be coming back from the gun show. So I backed out at the last minute, and I didn't go. I didn't want to go home yet, so I decided to go to Times Square in NYC. I found a new strip club, and I ended up spending most of my gun money. I started texting Mia from the club. I never told Mia the real reason why I went out that Saturday morning. I never told her I was contemplating suicide.

Saturday February 2, 2013, 3:01pm

Me: In NYC at gentlemans club

Mia: Which one?

Me: Don't know the name. It's near Port Authority. It's mostly white girls. Nice change from what I'm used to seeing at the other club I used to go to.

Mia: I was gonna text you to ask you where you were, but I didn't want to be intrusive

Mia: Get the name. I might want to go sometime

Me: Will do. It's 8 bucks admission.

Mia: Doable. Is it seedy though?

Me: No, looks good

Mia: Awesome

Mia: Did you get a lap dance?

Me: Yes

Mia: Sweet. I'm jealous.

Mia kind of has a bisexual mind, although I don't think she has ever been intimate with a woman—well, at least not to my knowledge.

Saturday February 2, 2013, 5:15pm

Me: On my way home now, smelling like a bunch of hot strippers

Mia: Wouldn't u like 2 bottle that smell?

Me: Wish I could live there. It was like I had 3 girlfriends

Suicide was still very much on my mind over the weekend, so much so that I decided that Monday February 4, 2013 was going to be my last day. Monday was normally a dialysis day, but because it was going to be my last day, I called the clinic and told them I wasn't coming in. Then I commuted to that new strip club again. I got there at around 1pm. I had a hard time enjoying myself though, because not going to dialysis was starting to catch up with me. One of the things that dialysis does is drain the body of excess fluids that damaged kidneys can't process. The longer you go without dialysis, the more those excess fluids can accumulate. The fluid starts getting in your lungs which leads to a lot of trouble breathing. That's what I was experiencing by the time I got to the strip club. It gets especially uncomfortable when you're sitting down because sitting compresses your airways. So I had to resort to getting my lap dances while standing up.

I managed to stay at the club for about 3 hours despite the fact that I felt so uncomfortable at times that I couldn't even get hard. I had used up all my gun money, and then I dipped into the money I had budgeted for my February living expenses/bills. When I left the club, the plan was to go back to the Port Authority Bus Terminal. From there I was going to take the subway to the Empire State Building, go to the highest possible floor, and jump to my death. The Port Authority was only a couple of blocks from the club, but I was having such breathing problems by then that every step was laborious. After every few steps I had to stop because I was literally gasping for air. Eventually I managed my way inside the Port Authority, and then I had a decision to make. I was hell-bent on getting to the Empire State Building to execute my suicide. However, I was feeling so lousy that ironically I didn't feel well enough to take the train and do the walking I would need to do to get there.

I had already bought a ticket for my bus ride home. I spent a long while sitting on a bench near where I was supposed to board my bus. I was wrestling with the question of, "Should I just go home, or should I muster up the strength somehow to commute to the Empire State Building?" After about 45 minutes, I decided I would just go home. The suicide would have to wait until another more suitable time. So the bus comes. I get on the bus and I realize within seconds after sitting down that I had to get up and off the bus. The brief little walk from the bench to the bus got me short of breath again. It was going to be about a 45 minute to 1 hour ride home. The trouble breathing was such an issue that I wasn't going to be able to sit for that long with my airways compressed.

I asked off the bus and sat on a railing right outside the bus. I was coughing like crazy, and then I started throwing up. The bus driver sent for paramedics who were on the premises at the Port Authority. They gave me some oxygen to help me breath and took my blood pressure, which was in the 220s. What ensued for the next several minutes is a fight between me and the paramedics. They were urging me to allow them to take me to the hospital, but I continued to refuse. After a while, they were able to convince me that I should go along with it. I let them strap me to a stretcher and wheel me to an elevator. I'm sure it was quite a scene to witness for all the commuters in the area. Then I asked the paramedics, "If I go to the hospital, how am I going to get back to the Port Authority so I can commute home?" They were like, "Oh it's only a few blocks, you can walk." That was enough to make me all uncomfortable about this going to the hospital thing again, so I demanded that they unstrap me because I changed my mind. I wasn't going.

They begrudgingly let me go. As we parted ways, one of them was like, "Ok, but if you collapse somewhere, remember that we tried to warn you." I somehow managed to get back to the waiting area for the next bus, and I was breathing well enough to be able to endure the long bus ride home. I think getting the oxygen had really helped. No one I came home to that evening would ever know how serious of a chance there was that they may have never seen me again after I had left that morning.

The thought of suicide has remained on my brain fairly regularly since that day. It's not something I'm planning anymore, but it's just something I think about. It's especially on my mind on a day when I start my dialysis treatment with a serious shortness of breath problem. On those days I know it's going to be at least an hour before the treatment kicks in, and in the meantime I'm in such agony because I'm gasping for air that I'm day dreaming about someone shooting me in the head to put me out of my misery. By the way, Wednesday February 6, 2013 was one of those days at dialysis. It had been five days since my last treatment, and way too much fluid had accumulated inside me over that period.

Wednesday February 13, 2013, 11:13am

Me: Every year it's one disaster after another with these cruises. Why do people continue to take them? Imagine the stink. People are having to dump in baggies and put them outside their rooms.

Reacting to the latest cruise disaster, the engine fire on the Carnival Triumph on February 10, 2013. Don't know why people love going on these cruises. But hey, I have a bit of a bias. I haven't traversed or even dipped a toe in a body of water in over 20 years, and I have no plans to either.

Thursday February 14, 2013, 8:13pm

Me: The Voltron witch was named Haggar.

Mia: I knew it started with an H

Mia and I were trying forever to remember that witch's name from the Voltron cartoon of the '80s. Turns out all I had to do was look up Voltron on Wikipedia.

Thursday February 21, 2013, 1:34pm

Me: Washing clothes right now. Which reminds me that Mr. Know it All had to ask me one day how to use the washer.

Mia: He still doesn't know how. Mom always has to wash his clothes. He's resistant to any modern technology. It's too complicated for his limited cranial capacity

This text exchange occurred only a couple of days after I had the biggest blowup ever with my father, who I referred to in the last text message as Mr. Know it All. My father had been getting on my nerves for a while since my move back home in January of 2012. After my hospital stays, it's like I was under his surveillance. He would stop by my room periodically at around midnight to see if I was asleep. If I wasn't, he'd start yelling at me about how he thought not getting enough sleep was making me sick. I know he meant well, but first of all, I was getting enough sleep despite being awake at midnight. Secondly, I'm a grown man. No one tells me what time to go to bed. He'd also make a big deal if he stopped by my room and caught me standing instead of sitting or lying down. Again, I'm a grown man. I'll stand if I want to stand.

I never reacted to any of his little lectures. I kept my sentiments to myself—like the time when he came in my room out of nowhere and lectured me about not refilling the toilet paper dispenser in the bathroom. I was this close to telling him where he could go for talking down to me like he did, but I swallowed it and let it go.

The big bone of contention became about the water bill and water usage. The water bill started going up when I came back to the house. Of course it would, because the house went from having two occupants to three. So over the course of 2012 and into 2013, this guy is needling me from time to time about using too much water to wash dishes. Actually, he never addressed me about the water usage directly. What he would do was make these snide comments about me in Creole while I would be in the same room washing dishes. I got tired of hearing it. I got tired of him thinking he could get away with making comments about me in Creole thinking I wouldn't understand.

It all came to a head one day in mid February of 2013 at around 6:30pm. I had just eaten, and I came downstairs to the kitchen with my dirty dishes. I had left a couple of small pots in the sink that I was going to wash as well. I couldn't wash my stuff right away because my father was already there washing his dishes. So I went to another room to wait for him to be done. I noticed that he was taking a long time, so I went back to the kitchen and found that he was starting to wash the stuff that I had left in the sink. As he was doing it, he was singing obnoxiously loudly and wasn't even acknowledging my presence.

I was thinking, "You can pretend that you're in your own little world all you want, but damn it you're gonna pay attention to me." So I looked directly at him washing my stuff and said, "You can leave that; I'll do the rest." He seemed to ignore me. So I said it again, very loud and very clear, "I said you can leave that; I'll do the rest!"

His initial response was a curt, "No." He was practically pouting as he said it. He was looking so childish. He was looking like a short, old, potbellied child. Then he goes, "What? So you can waste water and paper?" By paper, he was referring to the fact that I use paper towels to wash my dishes instead of a sponge. The reason I do that is because I feel like those sponges that get used over and over again are bacteria havens. With the paper towels, you use them for one dish washing and then you throw them away.

He finally begrudgingly steps aside from in front of the sink. I didn't like his attitude, and I just lost it. I shouted at him, "I'm the one that buys the paper, so I'll use as much as I want!" I guess he didn't like that I shouted at him—and I really exploded on him too—or he just didn't like being proven wrong. So perhaps out of spite, he gives me a real snarky low blow. He shouted at me that I was to blame for my kidney disease because of my eating habits. I shouted back at him, "You're not a doctor, you don't know anything!" I shouted it a second time for emphasis. I think I was so loud that I blasted him out of the room, and it felt pretty good too. I had been wanting to give it to him for a while, and I finally let him have it.

I spend a lot of time in my bedroom. I usually only come out to make food, go the bathroom or go out. He always seemed to have this misapprehension that just because he didn't see me *preparing a meal, it meant that I wasn't eating. He also had a stupid notion that I had made myself sick because I was on a no meat diet for a while. It may be true that my diet triggered my kidney disease, but not in the way my father perceives. My kidneys may have suffered from years of me eating large meals because I was obsessed with trying to gain weight. I was eating multiple servings of things which really piled on the sodium. I wasn't aware of how dangerous a high sodium intake was.*

After the blowup with my father, there was the aftermath. I came home from dialysis the next day, and he was in the kitchen when I opened the door. I made a split second decision to ignore him and head up to my bedroom. As of May 2014, I haven't spoken to him since and he hasn't spoken to me. I have no plans of breaking that routine. When we're in the same room, I pretend that he's not there and he does the same. He has to. I've given him no choice.

It really sucks though that I had to be reminded of him every time I used his car to drive to dialysis. Fortunately for 2013 I got a significant increase in my disability benefits. Although they took way my $150 a month of food stamps, my monthly disability check increased to about $1200 a month. So in 2013 I was feeling fairly optimistic about my chances of getting my own car, and maybe even a brand new car. However, my credit history created a potential roadblock.

Friday February 22, 2013, 10:31am

Mia: Happy Friday!! Got new Kindle yesterday

Me: Congrats!

Mia: Sorry. I meant to text Stan

Me: Congrats nonetheless

Mia: Thank you!

Sunday February 24, 2013, 1:48pm

Me: Mom looks like a cartoon character with those grey tights on. Big upper body and skinny legs syndrome.

For as long as I can remember, our mother has been top-heavy fat. She's about 5 foot 5 and 150 lbs, and all the weight is packed in from the ass up. Big flabby arms, sloppy mid section, meaty back, fat shapeless behind. And it's all supported by these skinny legs. Unfortunately, Mom is very open about showing her body. Mia and I have had the misfortune of seeing her walk around in her bra and big panties way too many times over the years.

Tuesday February 26, 2013, 1:10pm

Mia: Did UPS come yet?

Me: No

Mia: Text me when they come...please

Wednesday February 27, 2013, 3:51pm

Me: Guest whose iPad came today?

Mia: Hmmmm? Let me guess. Would that be mine? I did check UPS's website and it was delivered at 2:34. Thanks for the text. So excited. Won't be home till late though because I have counseling tonight.

Mia is having a very difficult time coping with having to live with the parents' again. I'm sure it's not lost on her that the year 2013 marks the 4th time since 1992 that she ended up coming back to the house after moving out. Mia told me also that she's seeing a therapist because she still bears psychological damage from when our uncle on our mother's side tried to rape her almost 30 years old when she was only 12. The fact that our mother didn't believe her and basically cross-examined her about it probably makes the memory of that incident that much harder to deal with.

Monday March 4, 2013, 11:18am

Me: Having a lot of trouble being on time for dialysis. My stomach has gotten slow so it's taking me longer to eat breakfast. I figure if I get up at 8:00 I can be on time. U think u can b done in the bathroom by 8 or as close to 8 as possible?

Mia: I understand that with your condition that you are likely to have certain physical limitations, such as the digestive issue. However, let's keep it real. And I'm not saying this to be mean or spiteful, just an observation. You already had issues getting to dialysis on time even before I moved back in the house and needed to use the bathroom in the am. But I will honor your request and try to be out of the bathroom by 8

Me: Thanks

Me: Not blaming u for being late. Just saying that I need to get in the bathroom earlier and that starts with me being consistent about getting up at 8. I've been having trouble doing that.

I had no idea that I would feel compelled to apologize for what I thought was a simple, no big deal request of my sister. It's like she thought I was blaming her for getting to dialysis too late. All I was asking was if she could be out of the bathroom by a certain time. I had a feeling she might get an attitude over it, which is why I texted the request instead of asking her face to face. How did she even know that I was struggling with lateness before she came back to the house? She wasn't around to witness it. Oh yeah, I forgot that she talks to Mom a lot and they'll talk about anything and everything—even though this is a woman Mia supposedly can't stand half the time.

Monday March 25, 2013, 4:18pm

Me: I'm gonna b chuckling now thinking of u every time I come home and see mom's car. Sorry, get ready to see it again when you get home today.

Mia: Yeah. At least I can laugh about it now. I'm fine as long as I know in advance, that way I can mentally prepare myself for the onslaught.

Mia: Did she cook by the way?

Me: Saw some fish in the works this morning. Not sure if it is done.

Mia: Ok thanks

In her adult years, Mia has had a very friendly relationship with Mom; but sometimes Mia's friendliness with Mom comes back to bite her. Mom loves to talk, and Mia really gets ticked off because Mom doesn't understand that there are certain times when she needs some space. When Mia comes home from work, if Mom is home, she'll often try to immediately engage Mia in conversation before she's had a chance to unwind after a long day. So when Mia comes home and sees Mom's car in the yard, she's not happy. Since the above text exchange, I've made sure to warn Mia before she gets home if Mom took a surprise day off.

Wednesday March 27, 2013, 11:46am

Me: They changed the dietician at the dialysis clinic. Nice that I no longer have to look at one of these women who thinks it's okay to sport a mustache.

Mia: Lol

Thursday April 11, 2013, 11:57am

Me: Your mom still has some smarts left. This morning she wanted to get off the home phone with someone who was talking her ear off, so she called the home phone with her cell phone.

Mia: Funny how her brain only functions properly for devious things

Mia: Why is Comcast coming to the house again? I got a call confirming a service appt last night

Me: Having slight problems with picture breaking up. Is your picture okay?

Mia: Yes. The breaking up does happen from time to time. That's a common occurrence with most cable providers

Wednesday April 17, 2013, 4:40pm

Mia: Did you wish your dademy a happy b-day today?

Me: Nope

Mia: And I guess you don't plan to

Me: You're funny.

"Dademy" was Mia's cool little amalgam of the words "dad" and "enemy." I was ignoring "dademy" since our huge blowup a couple of months earlier. I wasn't going to stop ignoring him to say "happy birthday."

Monday April 22, 2013, 11:56am

Me: Saw a humpback waltz into the yard last Thursday morning, i.e. a raccoon.

Mia: I'm trying to bite my lip to keep from laughing

Me: Thought they were nocturnal creatures. What's up with that?

Mia: Don't you hear them early in the morning on the roof?

Me: I may have heard some noises. Didn't think it was that. Had a nightmare back when I had my own place. Was taking out the garbage one night and all of a sudden noticed several raccoons up in the trees. A lot of sets of eyes glowing in the dark looking down at me.

Mia: That happened to me once at my old place. One night a pack of them ran out at me while I was taking the garbage out.

Me: Wow. We almost lost u. That's why I stopped taking trash out at night.

Mia: After that night, me too!

Monday April 22, 2013, 6:16pm

Me: RED ALERT. Mom's home and she's in the kitchen.

Mia: Lol! Thanks for the heads up

Just warning Mia who is minutes from coming home that Mom had the day off and she's in the kitchen. We just about always enter the house via the back door, and the kitchen is the first room you enter when you come in the house through the back door. Mom being in the kitchen meant that Mia would have to encounter her before she could get upstairs to her bedroom.

Friday April 26, 2013, 11:43am

Mia: If we chip in to get mom a new phone, what's the price limit?

Me: Give me an idea of what the price could be. Are we going the smart phone route?

Mia: I was considering a smart phone (def not an iPhone though). The two issues I have with getting her a smartphone are 1) she tends to be careless with her phone as far as leaving it at home when she's going out or misplacing it. So a smartphone is an expensive investment for someone who just may end up losing it. 2) she would have to pay an extra $30-$40 a month for a smartphone data plan. Not sure if she can afford that

Me: The other thing is having to walk her through the navigation of a more complex phone. Can we find something good for like 100 and we go 50/50? Do we want her to be able to text and take pictures?

Mia: Yessss. That thought occurred to me too, namely the tediousness of it. Especially since she isn't the most tech savvy. And yes, she should be able to take pictures and especially text. This way if we need to get in touch with her, we can do so without having to actually call her. I don't know what's available in the $100 price range. When you get home, can you go online and check some sites like AT&T or Best Buy and see what's in their inventory?

Me: Will do

Mia: Awesome

We were making plans to go out with Mom on Mother's Day 2013 to get her a new cell phone. We would end up spending about $200 and got her a Samsung Galaxy S3. It turned out to be kind of a regrettable purchase. It's really too bad that we couldn't have gotten her an iphone, but we didn't have enough money. We found that the Samsung was not nearly as user friendly as an iphone. Mia and I would take turns having little sessions with Mom to show her how to use the phone, but it was so different from the iphone that there was stuff that was hard for us to understand and explain to her. We had hoped we could show her how to text, but unfortunately it was too complicated for her. I just hope she's gotten comfortable enough with the phone so that in an emergency she at least knows how to make and receive calls.

Friday April 26, 2013, 5:09pm

Me: Just came home from the market to find an unfamiliar car in the driveway. I go inside and it turns out to be Teddy. Nice to see him I guess, but he's in the kitchen talking with Pop when

I'm getting ready to make food. Not a good time. An extra awkward social situation for me because of the presence of u know who.

"U know who" was a reference to our father, who we also refer to as "Pop" or "Pappy" or "the old man." Teddy is my godfather. Godparents are a big deal when you're a kid. My godparents were good for giving me toys and/or money for my birthdays. At this point it had been ions since I last saw or talked to Teddy. In my grown man years, he's just not a big deal to me anymore. He's not someone I think about much at all.

Mia: Teddy's there? Fuck!!!! Thanks for the warning. How long has he been there?

Me: Got home at about 5pm to find that surprise. Don't know how long he's been here.

Mia: That's another reason I was happy to have my own place. The parents always have company dropping in. Text me when he leaves

Me: U know I feel the same. I'll let u know.

Mia: And Teddy's just a bit too loud and boisterous. Not in the mood for that.

Me: Right I noticed that. When I got home he was talking about me all loud saying "look how tall he is and he's got a beard too!" As I'm shaking his hand I say, "I'm 36!"

Mia: LMFAO!!!!!

Mia: Yeah, they forget you're grown.

Mia: Or maybe because he's such a midget, you look like Paul Bunyan to him

Me: Yeah, he was sitting down when I came in so I must have looked to him like Shaq on chemo.

I was trying to make a pun based on the fact that I'm rather tall and thin. Don't think Mia got it.

Friday April 26, 2013, 6:02pm

Mia: Alright. Just walked out of work. Please tell me he's gone?

Me: Yes he is.

Mia: You sure???

Mia: Hellllllooooooo?

Me: Yesssssss

I was starting to make my food at the time Mia was texting me here, so I was distracted and there was a bit of an uncomfortable delay for Mia in terms of me taking a little too long to answer her "You sure???" text.

Monday May 6, 2013, 3:27pm

Me: Mom is home today. Sorry.

Mia: It's okay. This is her normal day off. So I'm mentally prepared. FYI though, she's off this Wed, which is not her typical day off

Mia: Good looking out, thx

Me: No problem

I don't like when Mom is home either. It's more annoying for Mia though. It's like as soon as a thought gets in Mom's head, she looks to engage Mia in conversation. I'm fortunate because Mom leaves me alone. Still it's annoying for me when she's home because she always talks so loud or is yelling about something, and I love quiet—as does Mia.

Mia: Did mom cook?

Me: She just finished mine. I assume she is working on everybody else's.

Mia: You sure?

Me: Yes

Mia: Thank you

Tuesday May 7, 2013, 11:16am

Mia: Your pappy pissed me the fuck off last night to the point where I started tearing up.

Tuesday May 7, 2013, 12:33pm

Me: Talk to me when u get home, unless u want to elaborate via text or email.

Mia: I'll talk to you when I get home. But here's the gist of it. He wants me and you to start paying the water bill beginning in June. I said NO

Me: Good. He's gotta fuck off with this water stuff. We r not the only fuckers that use water. I guess he thinks he's exempt cause he only washes his dirty ass once a week at best. Tired of having to use his car when half the time it smells like shit or unwashed ass.

Mia: I was so fucking pissed. It wasn't even a request. It was more like a command. That was the last straw that prompted me to move out the last time. As it is I give the parents $400 a month which puts a huge dent in my pocket. State Farm raised my car insurance because I moved back to the fucking ghetto. Last night when I got home, my car was smoking again and I have no money to get it fixed and this fucker wants to suck more money out of me. Not happening.

Mia: I have enough on my plate. I just fucking lost it last night. I have to get the fuck out of there, even if I have to live in my car (for however long my car lasts).

Me: He can't garnish our bank accounts. He can't force us to do shit. Try not to worry about it.

Mia: It's just one more thing among many. I'm stressed at work and then I have to be bullied at home. I'm gonna start looking for a place, even if it's just a room in someone's house

Me: Good luck. Go for it.

Despite Mia's anger in the last text exchange, as of May 2014 Mia is still living in the house. All the while she has continued to complain to me just about everyday about how sick she is of living with the parents. Sometimes I really wonder where her drive is to make necessary changes in her life. It's like her mind is willing, but her spirit is weak.

Wednesday May 8, 2013, 11:57am

Mother's Day is coming up on May 12th.

Me: Told mom not to make any plans after church on Sunday because we have plans for her. No turning back now.

Mia: Alright. Bet

Me: Bet? Haven't heard that expression in ions.

Mia: What did she say when you told her not to make plans? What was her reaction?

Me: Not overly enthused, but she said that would be nice. Why?

Mia: Would you want to take her to brunch after?

Me: No, just the phone.

Thursday May 9, 2013, 11:06am

Me: Sorry I shouted at you this morning. Thought it was one of the parents who was knocking on the door. I was thinking, "what the fuck could they possibly want to be disturbing me in the bathroom?" One time last year, mom came in on me in the shower just to tell me someone was calling me about my resume. That's great mom, but now is not the time. I think I remember her actually reaching into the shower to hand me the phone. I told her in a rather irritated tone, "take a message!" WTF

Mia: It's ok. No worries about this morning. I'd be a little miffed too if someone was knocking on the bathroom door if I was in there. And mom doesn't think before she acts. I can so picture her doing that to you.

Friday May 10, 2013, 11:14am

My PTI probation started in July of 2012. While the agreement called for a probation period of 3 years, I was hoping that if I could get all my required probation tasks completed early, I could get off probation early and be on my way to getting my charges expunged from my record. As of May 10th 2013, I had completed my community service requirement, I had paid my fines and I had just completed the required anger management course. The only thing left between me and potentially getting off probation early was getting the required psychiatric evaluation. I didn't think it was going to be a big deal, that is, until I ran into this doctor who seemed hell-bent on finding something wrong with me. I made sure to lie when he was interviewing me. If there were any questions he asked me where answering "yes" could indicate that I had issues, I made sure to answer those questions with "no"—like when he asked me if I had a tough upbringing. Still he felt like it was his job to find something wrong with me, in part because he kept thinking that the court would not have ordered a psychiatric evaluation unless they thought something was wrong with me. I tried telling him that the court ordered that just to give me a hard time, but he wasn't convinced.

I would end up seeing this doctor 3 times. In the end, he finally gave me the written report I was looking for that I could give to the court letting them know that I completed the psychiatric evaluation and nothing was wrong with me. Unfortunately what I got from this doctor was a report that included the following damning statement, "patient has been suffering from significant mood disturbances from 2009 to present, and therapy is recommended." I had told him I was depressed for a while after 2008 because I was struggling so much to find a job, but that doesn't mean I had issues. I was depressed for a reason. I would say I had issues if I was depressed for no apparent reason.

I was none too happy with that report, so I convinced my probation officer to allow me to seek another opinion from another doctor. I went to the psychiatric clinic of a local hospital. The hospital had me talk to two or three different people over a course of a 6 week period before I finally found somebody that put an end to this bullshit and gave me the report I needed that indicated there was nothing wrong with me. I didn't think the psychiatric evaluation was going to be a big deal. I started the process of getting one in May of 2013, and I would not be done with this task until early October of 2013. I had finally completed my probation requirements. Nevertheless, I was informed at the end of the year that the court was not going to grant me an early release from probation, and I had to wait until the term was over in July of 2015.

Me: Went for the psychiatric evaluation yesterday. This guy wants to see me again before he writes me the evaluation. Have to go back on the 30th. I was in the waiting room for 1.5 hrs before being called. I was subjected to watching ghetto tv, that is, Maury Povich followed by the Jerry Springer show. This doctor thinks I'm abnormally mellow. He thinks I have something called alexithymia, which makes u devoid of feelings. He wrote it down and asked me to look it up, and it took me a little while to find the term because he spelled it wrong. I'm supposed to take this guy seriously?

Mia: Where is this guy's office?

Me: Only a few blocks away from us.

Mia: Oh, so it's in the ghetto. No wonder u were subjected to ghetto tv.

Me: Actually I was doing my best to ignore the tv while I was in the waiting room. I was watching porn on my phone. This phone was my best purchase ever!

Mia: What site were u looking at?

Me: xvideos.com. No gay stuff for me unless it's 2 hot chicks.

Mia: That's ok. We all have different predilections. Watching gay guys fuck happens to be mine.

Mia: I'm a fag hag

Me: What ever gets u thru the day my friend.

Mia: I love it and I wear that monicker proudly.

Me: Amen. Hey Pop is getting up too damn early now. He was downstairs at 9:30 this morning. When I came down at 10:30 to wash my dish, he was in my way and I had to walk around him because he was foraging in the cabinet behind the sink. Then when he left the kitchen, he turned the light off without even asking. I was tempted to go off on him, but I'm not gonna give him the satisfaction of knowing that he's getting to me.

Mia: You mean, you were in the kitchen and he just turned the light off?

Me: Yep

Mia: That is so passive aggressive. Such bullshit

Mia: It's like he's trying to send a message that you do not exist to him.

Me: Fuck um. He doesn't exist to me either.

Wednesday May 22, 2013, 12:19pm

Me: Check out the tweet I emailed u from The Rock.

Wednesday May 22, 2013, 2:18pm

Mia: Unfortunately, I can't access my email here. But I'll check it out l8r

Me: Alrighty. When u do, click on the pic link

Me: Noticing a reduction in the water pressure of the shower. U think the old man adjusted something?

Mia: I wouldn't be surprised

Me: Is it just me? Have u noticed?

Mia: I noticed kinda when I was using the sink this am

It's our father's responsibility to pay the water bill. He's so obsessed with our water usage that I wouldn't have been surprised if he did something to reduce the water pressure.

Wednesday May 22, 2013, 4:26pm

Me: Finally out of jail. Just leaving dialysis now. Had to wait in waiting room for 1.5 hrs before starting cause they were surprised by inspectors. U have no idea how euphoric I am every Monday, Wednesday and Friday when I get to leave this place. It's like being on LSD. It's like getting out of jail.

Wednesday May 22, 2013, 5:34pm

Mia: I'm sure

Having to be on dialysis gives you a feeling of such a loss of freedom. It's not as bad as being in jail, but it's not that far removed either.

Thursday May 23, 2013, 5:34pm

Me: Sometimes I'll see that weird guy at the dialysis clinic that Pappy used to give money to. Yesterday was one of those days. He says to me, "say hi to your pops." "Ok," I said to him with a smile.

Of course that weird guy had no idea that I hadn't said a word to my father in about 3 months, and I had no intent on breaking the trend.

Friday May 24, 2013, 5:23pm

Me: Came home at about 5:10 to find mom cleaning cause somebody's looking at the house at 6:00. I'm getting ticked off. She was telling me to tidy up stuff. I had left a plate and a pot on the couch in my room. When I came home, I found that she had put the plate and the pot on the floor behind the couch for some reason. WTF? So now I gotta wait for these fuckers to come and go before I can eat cause I don't want people poking their heads in my room while I'm eating. So ticked off!

Mia: Fuck!!! I didn't even clean my room. So that means she's gonna be all up in it if she hasn't been already. Just when I think I'm just gonna come home and chill. Sick of this already. Again, I say, I miss my friggin apartment

Mia: Thanks for the heads up

Me: Not totally on board with selling the house. What if we do the reverse mortgage thing? Wouldn't we be able to stay in the house and the parents could move to Florida?

Mia: I just don't want to be the one solely responsible for all that house. And I don't want to keep living in the hood

Me: Yeah, you're right about that.

Friday May 24, 2013, 6:13pm

Mia: Did the house visitors come and go yet?

Mia: And I know mom will draw out the visit longer than necessary given how much she likes to gab

Me: I think the people are still here.

Mia: Where? I'm in my car parked a few blocks away.

Mia: Have they been upstairs already at least?

Me: Actually they just left.

Mia: Thank you. You rock!

Me: Hey, u know I feel ya more than any other.

At this point, Mom has been futilely trying to sell the house since 2009. It really infringes on our space when potential buyers come over to look at the house. Instead of selling, Mom was also weighing the reverse mortgage idea that could potentially allow her to abandon the house and go to Florida with our father. For that to be viable, Mia and I might have to remain living in the house indefinitely for maintenance purposes.

Monday May 27, 2013, 12:45pm

Me: Hope mom hasn't been too irritating today.

Mia: No less than usual, counting the minutes.

This is was a day when Mia had the day off, and she's counting down the minutes until 2pm when Mom leaves for work.

Me: Any mention of mangos today?

Mia: Surprisingly no

The day before, Mom got a great deal at this little market on mangos, and she couldn't stop talking to Mia about it. She was driving her nuts.

Mia: When will you be home?

Me: Bout 3:15

Mia: Oh ok. Cause when she leaves, then it's only me and the old man in the house. I need u to be my buffer.

Me: Hang in there buddy.

Mia: Will do. Any sign of the homeless guy today?

Me: U mean the guy that pop gives cash?

Mia: Yeah

Me: Don't think he's homeless, and I haven't seen him.

Mia: He's not homeless but he's bummin for change?

Me: He doesn't bum 4 it, but pop feels 4 some reason that he's got to hook him up

Mia: Really. No wonder he told you to say "hi" to your pop.

Me: Absolutely

Wednesday May 29, 2013, 1:31pm

Mia: Hey Bill. On your way home, do you think you can pick me up some diet ginger ale? Not feeling good. Didn't go to work today

Me: Ok, hang in there.

Mia: Thanks

Thursday May 30, 2013, 3:36pm

Me: You know your mother's home right?

Mia: Yes. Good lookin out though

Mia: Did mom cook? I'm guessing no

Mia: Hello?

Me: No. Sorry, I was away from the phone cooking.

Mia: So no food

Me: No food

I've gotten the idea that my sister's job has led her to develop very poor eating habits. It doesn't seem like she eats much at all during the day—rarely has a breakfast or a lunch—and by the end of her day she's starving. Then it becomes a real let down for her when she learns that Mom didn't cook. She should do what I learned to do and cook her own food, but it's not something she feels like doing when she gets home. Then she'll end up eating pre-prepared frozen garbage that you just have to pop in the toaster oven—like pizzas and french fries. Mia has had a number of overweight periods over the years. At the end of 2009, she was in the best shape I can ever remember her being in. Since she moved back into the house in 2013, I can see that she may be approaching her all-time highest weight. As of May 2014 she must weigh about 170 lbs, and she's not very tall at 5 foot 5. It's hard to look at how she's let herself go. Again, I wonder where her motivation is.

Wednesday June 5, 2013, 11:11am

Me: Looking at autotrader.com to get a used car. Would u want to go to the dealership with me on Saturday afternoon? Not sure where yet.

Mia: Sure

Me: Excellent!

Thursday June 6, 2013, 2:36pm

Me: Just made appointment with a Ford dealership on Route 440 for Saturday at 2pm. Looking at a 1999 Toyota Camry for $4000 that's got 74000 miles

Mia: Cool

Thursday June 6, 2013, 4:31pm

Mia: Did mom cook?

Me: Yes

Mia: Just for you?

Me: No, 4 everyone

Mia: Groovy

If Mom cooks for me, she has to cook my stuff separately from everyone else's. I'm on a very low sodium diet due to my kidney disease, so I ask Mom to cook my chicken with no added salt. By this point I had learned how to cook for myself, but sometimes Mom does me the favor of cooking for me anyway. That's really helpful sometimes because when I come home from dialysis, I really don't feel like doing much of anything. But if she doesn't cook for me, then I just grin and bear it and do my own cooking.

Me: I was walking just a couple of blocks away from the house and passed by some new townhouses that made me say, "Am I still in the ghetto?"

Mia: Yeah I saw those. It's only a matter of time before the ghetto riffraff that move in mess them all up

Me: Sadly, you're probably right about that.

Saturday June 8, 2013, 2:57pm

On this day I'm finally getting my own car. It wasn't fun having to drive the car of someone that I hate—my father. I hadn't had a car since my 2007 Pontiac G6 was repossessed back in December of 2011. Here's the text exchange between Mia and I when I was in the dealership and she decided to wait for me outside in her car.

Mia: Gonna just chill in the car. Come out when u r done.

Me: Ok

Me: U ok hanging in the car? Don't know how long it'll take to get a deal.

Mia: I'm starving and I gotta pee. What's going on now?

Me: I was told it would be about a 15 minute wait to process my application for a lease. Meantime, come back here and u could pee and get something from a vending machine.

Mia: Nope. You know me and public restrooms, and no on the vending machine. I'm cool. They always tell you 15 min and you end up being there 5 hours

Me: If you really have to pee you could just squat next to the car. JJ

Saturday June 8, 2013, 3:35pm

Still at the dealership

Mia: Where r we now?

Me: Still waiting for the application process, but the salesman sounded confident that I'd be approved. Took a walk with the guy to see the ford. Looks good.

Mia: Ok

I went to the dealership with my eye on a 1999 Toyota Camry with 74000 miles on it. I thought I could finance it, but the banks won't provide a loan for cars that old. Then the salesman says that he could get me a lease deal on a new 2013 Ford Fiesta. I was at the dealership for over 4 hours. I told Mia that she could go home without me because I was really confident that I was going to be able to drive myself home in a new car, and that's exactly what I ended up doing. The odds were against me at the start of the day. I had filed for bankruptcy the year before, I wasn't working, and I only had $1200 a month in disability income. Still when I left for the dealership with Mia that day, I was so confident that I would be coming home in my own car that I brought the club, the snow removal brush and the ezpass tag from my previous car because I believed I would have a new car to put them in.

Mia seemed to question whether I should be so confident, but you have to think positively. One of the problems I have with Mia is that she's too negative, too pessimistic. Mia's got this beat up car that's over 10 years old that's always giving her problems. I told her that if I could get a deal on a new car, then she should at least call my Ford dealership to inquire about the possibility of getting her own deal on a new car. As of May 2014, 11 months after I got my new car, Mia is still driving that old headache of a car. She filed for bankruptcy in 2013 and she's apparently been waiting to receive her official discharge letter. She's been waiting months for that letter. I told her to forget about that. Just contact my dealership and explain your situation and see if they can work with you. But she hasn't done that. She's just content with continuing to wait for this discharge letter. She also came up with the excuse that she doesn't trust Fords because Ford happens to be the manufacturer of her current car that she's had so much trouble with. Nevertheless, I don't consider a Ford really a Ford if it does not have the Ford trademark on it, and Mia's Mercury Cougar does not have the Ford trademark. Anyway, what I told her in response to her reservations about Ford was that "beggars can't be choosers."

Friday June 14, 2013, 2:12pm

Mia: I think ya mammy isn't going to work today.

Me: Ok. Looking forward to seeing that big blue car when I get home. Thx.

Mom drives a midnight blue Jeep Liberty SUV.

Mia: I'm a little annoyed. Not what I needed today

Me: I know. Tough day for u to have to stay home.

Mia: Yes. Especially while I'm not feeling well

Monday June 17, 2013, 4:33pm

Mia: Bill. I have to pick up my car from the mechanic after work. Can you come with me? I have pop's car and I can't drive 2 cars back.

Me: Ok. You'll be home around 6:30 as usual?

Mia: Yes

Me: Alright

Tuesday June 18, 2013, 12:37pm

Me: 2014 on the Disney Channel, get ready for Girl Meets World! The show will revolve around 12 yr old Riley and her friend Maya entering 7th grade. Riley's parents will b none other than Cory and Topanga! Cory is a teacher at the school. Topanga runs this pudding shop where all the kids like to hang out. Cory's old floppy haired friend Shawn might b in the picture as well. Lookin forward to checking this out.

Tuesday June 18, 2013, 1:38pm

Mia: Hmm. I'd like to see how the original Boy Meets World cast members look like all grown up

Me: Yeah that'll be real interesting to see them grown up and with kids of their own.

Friday June 21, 2013, 3:50pm

Me: Your mom is a trip. The other day I come downstairs to do my oatmeal at around noon, a tad later than usual. She's in the kitchen and she's like "What happened today, did u wanna sleep a little more?" I didn't even acknowledge the question. Then she's like "nothing wrong with wanting to sleep a little more, that's okay." Her tone the whole time was friendly, but still though, I wasn't looking for her approval of my coming downstairs to eat at a certain time.

Mia: I feel you.

Living with these parents can feel like being under constant surveillance. You feel like they're always at the ready to scrutinize and critique and make comments about everything you're doing.

Monday June 24, 2013, 1:58pm

Me: Bold and the Beautiful is some good shit. Only 25 minutes, flies by and they get a lot of stuff in. Lot of fun.

I've become a big Bold and the Beautiful fan in 2013. My mother is a big fan of the show as well, but I have yet to indicate to her that I watch it. I don't want to give her something that she will always try to talk to me about. I don't necessarily hate my mother, but I'm not looking to be her friend either.

Wednesday June 26, 2013, 4:54pm

Mia: Lately your pappy has been hanging out in the kitchen. Everyday when I come home, he's there. Bad enough I know he's there, but before I even get out of my car, he has already opened the back door. It's a cramped kitchen. He's all in the way, and then I have to squeeze around him while I'm carrying my shoulder bags.

Me: Idk what's going on with him. I feel your pain.

Mia: I bet he's in the kitchen now. Probably waiting for me to come home.

Me: He was in the kitchen when I got home at around 4. He was washing dishes. He went upstairs at around 5.

Mia: I'm sure he'll be back down there by the time I get home. I swear he plans these things

Wednesday June 26, 2013, 5:13pm

Me: He just went downstairs a few minutes ago. He went to the basement.

Mia: Ok thanks for the update

Friday June 28, 2013, 4:39pm

Me: Happy "Your Father is Showering Day!"

Our father showers once a week at best, and even less frequently in the winter time. Btw, you'll notice in our texts to each other that my sister and I often refer to our parents as "your mother" or "your mammy," or "your pappy." Or instead of referring to them as "mom" or "pappy," we'll sometimes refer to them just as "he" and "she" or "him" and "her." It's just an illustration of how little regard we have for those two. We've always wanted different parents, and sometimes in protest we refuse to take ownership of our current ones.

Wednesday July 3, 2013, 6:58pm

Me: I Love Lucy marathon tomorrow from 9am to 9pm on ch. 810

Mia: Thank you☺

Tuesday July 9, 2013, 5:26pm

Mia: Is your pappy downstairs in the kitchen? He's doing that annoying "perched on the stool at the sink/counter thing" again. I was pissed off last night when I came home and he opened the door for me

Me: He's in the basement as of now. When are the parents leaving for vacation and when are they coming back?

Mia: They're leaving on 8/3 and coming back 8/17. Can't fucking wait. I wish mom would just leave the old man down there

Wednesday July 10, 2013, 1:19pm

Mia: I was driving to work this morning thinking about "you got served." So proud of you and mom for shutting him up! Everyday it baffles me that such an ignorant, intellectually challenged man fathered me

Me: Couldn't wait to tell u about it. Boy did it feel good. Wish I could've taped it and showed u.

The day before this text exchange, I was provoked into breaking my silence with my father—Mr. Know it All. He thinks he's so slick. I was washing my dishes after eating breakfast, and he's in the kitchen talking to my mother in Creole. He turns the subject of his conversation to me. He starts making comments about the manner in which I was washing the dishes, but of course he's doing it while speaking Creole because he still stupidly thinks that I don't understand the language. So I interrupt him while he's talking about me in Creole. I look directly at him and I'm like, "You don't think I understand what you're saying? How many times do I have to tell you that I understand you when you're speaking in Creole? Stop trying to be sneaky. If you wanna talk about me, just do it in English. And I don't wash dishes your way, I do it my way."

Surprisingly, my mother backed up my sentiments and gave my father her two cents as well. It's hard to fully capture and describe the moment in writing, but my father was stunned by my little rant. In fact, he was so stunned that from the point when I interrupted him talking to my mother to the point when I left the room, he did not say another word.

Wednesday July 10, 2013, 5:09pm

Me: Just came downstairs to cook. Just as I was hoping that he wouldn't b in the kitchen, he was going out right as I entered the kitchen. Life's good sometimes.

Mia: Yes it is, at least for you. I'm sure he'll be back just in time to open the door for me

"He" is in reference to our father.

Monday July 15, 2013, 4:07pm

Me: I think mom just got news that a relative died and she's wailing. Was there anybody u knew of that was sick?

Mia was so concerned that she actually called me. And she hates talking on the phone. She asked me to go to Mom to find out what's wrong. I reluctantly went to Mom's bedroom only to find that she was wailing because she was taking a nap and was having a bad dream. My sister was not happy, as she was interrupted from work for something that she thought was serious. Our Mom can be such a drama queen.

Me: I didn't mean to alarm u, but last time I heard her making sounds like that, I was used to it meaning that somebody died. Turns out she was just reacting to a bad dream she was having that somebody in the house was trying to kill her.

Ironically, Mia had recently shared with me that she had envisioned herself killing the parents. The way she was describing that vision to me was a little disturbing. She made me wonder if she could actually be capable of doing it. I told her somewhat facetiously that if she ever went through with the murders, she should not bank on me protecting her because I'm not going to jail for her. I told her if she ever went through with it, flee the crime scene immediately and don't try to contact me because I want nothing to do with it.

Monday July 15, 2013, 5:42pm

Mia: Is all quiet now?

Me: Yes. All the dramatics are over.

Mia: Good. Don't need to be subjected to any hysteria when I'm just getting home from work. Oh and FYI, she's off this Friday

Mia: Is she asleep?

Me: She is in the kitchen

Wednesday July 17, 2013, 5:24pm

Mia: Where's ya pappy?

Me: Basement probably

Mia: Ok. Good

Mia: Don't 4get, mom is off tomorrow. So she'll be home for the next 3 days

Me: Looking forward to it. Tee-hee

Mia: Dreading it. She doesn't cling to you

Me: Yeah, but I like a quiet house as much as you. I'm gonna b missing that.

I've mentioned this before, but I'll mention it again. Mia has been way too friendly and conversational with our mother over the past several years. As a result, Mom doesn't give Mia enough space and looks to engage her in conversation about anything that comes to her mind. Mia's in a predicament that she kind of created. When she was living on her own from 2010 to 2012, I'll never understand why she was spending entire weekends at the parents' house. It was making me look like the bad guy when I was living on my own and I rarely visited the house and only called the house like every two to three weeks at best. My mother would call me and she'd be like, "Oh we never see you, you rarely call. Mia calls every week and even spends weekends with us." She was basically saying, "Why can't you be more like your sister?" I don't think I ever gave her an answer, but I was always thinking, "I'm gonna do what I do. I don't live by what Mia does."

Friday July 26, 2013, 12:01pm

Me: U okay? U were home when I left.

Mia: My boss called me and asked me if I wanted to use my personal day today. All employees have to use any personal time they have accrued by 8/3. I didn't even think twice when she asked me because I'm not feeling well today.

Me: Okay. 8/3 is a big day for a couple of reasons.

August 3rd is the beginning of our parents' two week vacation trip, and the beginning of our long awaited vacation from having to live with those two.

Friday July 26, 2013, 2:05pm

Me: Knock knock joke: knock knock

Mia: Yessss

Me: U have to say who's there.

Mia: I know. Who's there?

Me: Anthony Weiner... the end

Mia: Huh??

Me: Not familiar with this guy? If not just google his name

Mia: Wasn't he this disgraced politician?

Me: Yes. Google him or better yet look him up on Wikipedia.

Mia: Ok. Oh tonight @ 7:30 on TV One (Channel 173) is the What's Happening Doobie Bros episode, part 1

Me: Thx. Btw, the funny with Weiner is that his last name is pronounced like the nickname for a penis. And he keeps dissing his wife by sexting women and sending them pics of his weiner!

Mia doesn't watch the news enough. Still I was actually a little shocked that she wasn't really familiar with Anthony Weiner. At this time he was being talked about everyday because he was running for NYC mayor amidst a sexting scandal. I had a conversation with Mia recently in which she admitted to me that she felt intellectually inferior to me because I know a lot more than she does about what's going on in the world and in politics. Earlier this year Mia and I got into the subject of a woman potentially becoming President. I mentioned how we had a chance to get one in 2008, but we chose Obama instead. I remember how surprised I was that it was news to Mia that Hillary Clinton had already run in 2008.

In response to Mia's feeling of intellectual inferiority, I told her that I'm not that smart. I just keep myself abreast of what's going on by watching the news, MSNBC and Real Time with Bill Maher.

Tuesday August 6, 2013, 2:41pm

Me: Called the alarm company yesterday. The account is now with ADT. Would have to schedule a tech to come and reprogram the alarm with a new code. Would love to call and set this up, but they charge 25 bucks. Do u have that? I'm tapped out.

Mia: They can't reprogram it remotely? 25 bucks doesn't factor into my budget after buying food

Me: No they have to send somebody over.

It's the 3rd day into our parents' vacation. For times when my sister and I are both out and the house is left empty, I wanted to be able to activate the alarm. Our parents have an active ADT account, but they could never activate the alarm because they forgot the passcode. So I took it upon myself to call ADT to try and get a new passcode so we could feel more secure about leaving the house empty. We don't live in a good neighborhood. Our house was broken into at least twice in the past, although the last time was around 1993.

Friday August 16, 2013, 2:22pm

Me: Give me an idea of where to find okra at Shoprite

Mia: Frozen foods or the produce aisle

Me: Thanks

Mia: No prob

Monday August 19, 2013, 1:06pm

Mia: My car wouldn't start this morning.

Me: Wow. What r u thinking about doing?

Mia: I have no idea, but I may need a ride to work tomorrow

Me: Any day u can't get the car from dad, u can use mine. May need help with gas if this becomes a regular thing though. I'm living check 2 check now. Money is tighter than ever.

Mia: No problem. It just may be a regular thing at least for the next couple of weeks. And gas is a non issue. I get it

Me: Ok. Maybe tonight we can take a spin around the block so u can get to feeling comfortable behind my wheel.

Mia: Ok sounds good

Me: U realize this is only a Tuesday Thursday thing. U comfortable with bouncing back and forth between my car and pop's car?

I have to use my car on Mondays Wednesdays and Fridays to get to dialysis.

Mia: I guess I don't have a choice.

Me: Thinking about what 2 do with your old ride in the meantime. U may have to ask Willie if he can do something to get it started. Or if u have triple A, u could see if they could send somebody 2 look at it or have it towed 2 a mechanic. U at least need a diagnosis.

Willie is our next door neighbor.

Mia: I guess I'll call AAA and have them tow it to Firestone

Me: No problem with u driving mine, but wouldn't it b easier 2 ask pop if u could drive his car everyday til yours is fixed instead of bouncing back and forth between his car and my car? He's not working. Where does he have to go?

Mia: We'll talk later

I can't lie. I did not want Mia driving my car. It was nothing against Mia. I'm just not comfortable with anyone driving my car. Nevertheless, it does make more sense for her to be driving the same car everyday instead of my car today and Pop's car the next day.

Tuesday August 20, 2013, 11:36am

Mia took my car to work on this day.

Me: B careful when driving my car up inclines/hills. When u have to stop at the top of a hill, the car can roll back during transfer of foot from brake to gas when the stop is over. Transfer should be done quickly especially if someone is stopped close behind you.

Mia: Yeah. I noticed that this morning. Just like pop's car

Me: Also look at the warning lights after you start my car because that'll remind u if the parking brake is on.

Mia: Yes dear

Me: Alright snookums

Mia: Lol

Mia: But it is a sweet little ride. I'm on your Ford dealership's website right now

Me: Good.

Me: Willie checked out your car. He has an idea about what's wrong. He was able to drive it around the block.

Mia: He got it to start?

Me: You're funny. I said he was able to drive it around the block.

Mia: I know, that was a DUH moment. Actually more like a mom moment. I just wasn't expecting him to be able to get it started let alone drive it.

A "mom moment" is in reference to our mother's propensity for saying the dumbest things.

Me: How would Dorothy from the Golden Girls reply to that question?

Mia: "No Rose, since he couldn't get it to start, he just road the engine bareback."

Me: Lol. That was good.

Me: Is mom working today?

Mia: No. She's not going back to work until Sept 2

Me: Omg! That news gave me the Macaulay Culkin "Home Alone" face. Unbelievable.

Mia: Why? Is she driving you nuts?

Me: Not right now cause I don't think she's here. Sept 2? Wow. 2 more weeks of noise

Boy I swear... I know Mom bothers Mia a lot because she's always talking her ear off while she leaves me alone, but Mia doesn't appreciate how much Mom's sheer presence bothers me as well. Sometimes it's like she has the monopoly on being sick of our mother, and I'm not allowed to feel the same way.

Friday August 30, 2013, 4:06pm

Mia: Are u home?

Me: Just got home.

Mia: Is mom home?

Me: No

Mia: Ok thanks

Mia: With my luck, by the time I get home, she will be

Me: Well at least Sept. 2nd is right around the corner.

Mia: Yes!! Counting the fucking minutes until she goes back to work.

Me: I know she doesn't bother me as much as she bothers you, but it's her sheer presence that bothers me. Day after day after day, she's here. Not something u can get used to.

Mia: Tell me about it. And you're right about her bothering me more than you

Mia: And notice she's back to yelling across the hall again

Our mother's room and my sister's room are about 15 to 20 feet apart on opposite ends of the second floor of our house. Mom talks so loud—and she gets lazy I guess—so sometimes if she has something to say to Mia, she'll shout it across the hall instead of going to her room.

Me: Has that ever stopped? It's a fine line 4 u. If you're less inviting to her in a way that discourages her from talking to u, she'll call u on it. U surprised me last Saturday morning. U were in her room a long time.

Mia: Yes because every time I tried to get up to leave, she was like "come on, stay." She just kept on talking

Mia: And believe me, I try to be as uninviting as possible, but the more aloof I try to be, the more needy she gets

Mia: And I'm sick of her bipolar moods

Me: I don't know how u would say to her that there are times when u need some space without her getting mad. But sometimes u gotta b sort of direct and cut conversations short. Last Saturday u were in her room for well over an hour. At some point u should b allowed to say without actually saying it, "mom, I gave u enough time. I gotta go now."

I'm trying to convey to Mia that she has to be less friendly if she wants our mother to talk to her less and give her more space. Here's where my sister gets really bizarre. On the rare occasions when Mom is not in a talking mood and Mia tries to talk to her and gets terse and surly responses, Mia gets mad and complains to me that Mom's acting anti-social towards her. She refers to it as Mom being in one of her bipolar moods. But Mia, I thought you wanted her to leave you alone? It's a rare time when she doesn't feel like talking your ear off, and you're complaining about it? Huh?

It would be one month until our next text exchange. During this time, Mia and I had a falling out. We have a back yard where we park our cars, and the yard is closed off by a fence with a large gate. There was a time when we would leave that gate closed all day. When someone had to go out, they would open the gate so they could drive out, then get out of their car and close the gate behind them before they took off to wherever. In recent years however, it became the routine to leave the gate open all day and have it closed overnight.

One day in late August of 2013, I was in the kitchen and I could see through the window that a couple of high school kids just wondered into the yard and walked a circle around my car. They left the yard after 20 seconds or so, but obviously I was not comfortable after seeing these kids looking like they were casing my new car. I believed that if it wasn't for the open gate, they would not have been compelled or tempted to come into the yard. Therefore I told Mia and our mother—and our mother relayed the message to our father—that we had to start leaving the gate closed from then on because the open gate was an invitation.

Mia was on board with the idea of keeping the gate closed, that is, until it directly affected her. She didn't want the hassle of having to close the gate behind her when she went off to work in the morning, and then having to get out of her car and open the gate when she got home so she could come in the yard. So I told her that I would ease her pain and meet her halfway. I told her that when she's coming home and is a couple of blocks away from the house, she could call me and I would come outside and open the gate for her. I told her that she was on her own with the gate in the morning, but I'd be there for her in the afternoon. She seemed okay with the idea. I thought we had an agreement, a compromise. Yet I was noticing that day after day she was leaving the gate open after driving off to work in the mornings.

I thought it was pure laziness on her part. So after a week or so of opening the gate for her in the afternoon, I staged a little protest. She called me one afternoon to come outside to open the gate, but I ignored the call. Thus she actually had to open the gate herself so she could come in the yard. Then she came upstairs and stopped by my room. She addressed me in a lighthearted way as she asked me where I was. I just told her that I wasn't going to be at her beckon call anymore. She was really miffed by that response and left my room in a huff as she said, "Alright, fuck it!"

We went without speaking for a while after that, and then there was an encounter I had with her and our mother that made things worse. Mom also had a problem with having to close the gate behind her all the time when she went out. Mia was agreeing with her, so it was the two of them against me. I guess I made the mistake of saying that having a problem with closing the gate was just being lazy, which they both took umbrage with. Maybe I shouldn't have gone there, but I think I was right nevertheless.

After a few uncomfortable weeks of not being on speaking terms with Mia, I went to her and apologized for intimating that she was being lazy—even though that's exactly what she was showing herself to be—and I agreed to go back to opening the gate for her when she gets home from work. Over the years when my sister and I have had periods when we were not on good terms, it seems like it has always been me that breaks the silence and apologizes.

Tuesday October 1, 2013, 4:17pm

Mia: I have to stop somewhere before I get home. I'll be home before 6. Will u still b downstairs in the kitchen?

Me: I may be upstairs but I'll get out to u right away.

Mia: Thanks. Just wanna get something to eat before I come home. I'm starved and I know mom didn't cook. And when pop sees me downstairs cooking, he's all up in my business, sniffing around like he wants some

Me: Sniffing. He is rather primitive and animal like isn't he?

Mia: I just chuckled to myself

At this point, Mia is home from work by around 5:30pm everyday. So I started timing when I cooked my dinner so that I would be downstairs in the kitchen when she calls me to come outside and open the gate for her. She was letting me know that her call would be coming later than usual.

Thursday October 10, 2013, 1:16pm

Me: Mom called in sick.

Mia: Word? Good lookin out

Monday October 21, 2013, 4:28pm

Mia: What's mom up to?

Me: Applying heat stimulation to her knees.

Mia: No food then?

Me: No

Wednesday October 30, 2013, 12:48pm

Mia: How r u doing? Mom said you were throwing up this morning?

Me: Drank a little too much water yesterday so I got fluid in my lungs. Feeling better, I'm having more fluid removed than usual at dialysis so my lungs will get cleared.

Mia: Ok, sorry.

Me: Hey that's life.

The hardest thing about dealing with kidney failure is following the very restrictive diet you have to be on. You have to take in as little sodium as possible, and sodium is in just about everything you see at the market. You have to avoid foods that are high in phosphorus, and you have to consume a lot of protein. It's tricky because much of the high protein food has a lot of phosphorus and sodium. The worst thing is the fluid restriction. Drinking a lot of water is good for you, but not so if you have kidney failure. I get so thirsty sometimes and my mouth and throat get so dry, but I can't over indulge in water or I run the risk of developing serious breathing difficulty because fluid can build up in my lungs.

Me: Do u know if mom is going to the hospital?

Mia: She went to see her internist. I told her that would be better than the ER. He'll probably send her for an MRI which would be her best option at this point

Me: Might have to get that knee aspirated.

Mia: We'll see. I think she's at the doctor's office right now. She had a 12:00 appointment

Me: Pretty uncomfortable to witness yesterday. Lucky u missed it. She was in so much pain that she was wailing like somebody died.

Mia: Believe me. I'm glad I missed it

Me: I know u've got issues with your job, but b thankful u had it yesterday.

Mia: I am. I'm not insensitive to suffering, but I have zero tolerance for histrionics

I mentioned earlier about how our mother can be a serious drama queen, and I was texting Mia about an example of that. Mom works a lot of double shifts. Her normal shift is 3pm to 11pm, then she doesn't come home and works a second shift from 12am to 8am. Her double shifts really caught up with her yesterday. She tried to get up from a nap at around 1pm to get ready for work, but one of her knees was swollen to twice its normal size. She was wailing and screaming because it hurt with every step and she was having immense trouble straightening her leg. Although I hated the idea of her staying home, I had to tell her that she should call in sick. So she called her supervisor and she's bawling uncontrollably on the phone with her for several minutes about how much pain she was in. For the rest of the day, she was wailing and screaming with every step she tried to take. She would end up getting an MRI and it revealed that she had a cyst in her knee, and she was given some medication that would get rid of the swelling. She would have to take a week off from work, unfortunately for Mia and me.

Friday November 1, 2013, 10:45am

Mia: How are u feeling?

Me: Good. Got 2 consecutive nights of good sleep finally. For over a month I had been sleeping 2 hrs or less and having trouble breathing cause of too much fluid in my lungs. I think the fluid is finally gone. My alarm clock woke me up for the first time in weeks.

Mia: Good. Mom is driving me nuts. She's supposed to be off her feet and she was bitching that she was in all this pain because she cooked yesterday. When I reminded her that she was supposed to be resting, she snaps at me talking about, "Well I'm hungry. Who's gonna feed me?!" After the day I had at work yesterday, that was the last thing I needed. Then she copped an attitude when I snapped at her

Me: She told me on Wednesday that she would cook for me on Friday (today). I said, r u sure? She said it was ok. Guess I should tell her I'll do it myself, but I don't want telling her that to start an altercation. You never know with her. When she's off from work, she doesn't relax enough. She does too much moving around.

Me: Another thing. She has got to find a way to get rid of some of that upper body gristle. Too much weight on those cartoon-like skinny legs puts too much stress on her knees.

Mia: Lol

Mia: I'm sitting here trying not to burst out laughing

Mia: Have you heard about the cyber attack drill?

Me: No. What have u heard?

Mia: Just google cyber attack drill November

Me: I just looked it up. Here's what I found. Apparently our power grid is too vulnerable to terrorist attack. If it gets attacked, we're fucked cause the grid keeps everything running. If it goes down, no electric, no gas, no fuel, no communications, no water. All the utility companies that run the grid (made up of over 5800 power plants) are working with the government to simulate an attack on the computer systems that control the grid. Some ppl in Congress, probably Democrats, want more regulations in place to make utility companies reinforce the defenses of their computer systems/equipment. Sounds like Republicans don't agree with this cause they think regulations hurt business, even though many of the utility companies said they would be willing to cooperate with stricter security standards. Bottom line, can't worry about it. There's too much other stuff to worry about already.

Mia: Eloquently stated

Me: Thanks

Mia: You just summarized the situation so clearly

Me: About an hour ago somebody just walked into LAX airport with a rifle. When he got to a checkpoint, he opened fire. So the airports are good at keeping ppl from boarding planes with weapons, but apparently nothing's stopping anyone from walking into the airport building itself with a gun.

Saturday November 2, 2013, 12:06pm

Mia: Hey did the house hunters come by yet?

The seemingly futile exercise of trying to sell the house continues.

Me: Not yet

Mia: Seriously? What are the elders up to?

Me: Father is out. Mom is cooking potatoes.

Mia: Ok, cool

Mia: Text me when the home visit is over

Me: Ok

Saturday November 2, 2013, 3:42pm

Me: Coast is clear.

Mia: Thank you

Tuesday November 5, 2013, 11:56am

Me: You need to be more anti-social with your mother, but don't be too obvious about that cause she'll notice and call u out on it. Cut down on the words between u 2 and there'll be less opportunity for her to say something to tick u off. You can't trust her. U never know what u say to her that will set her off 4 some reason. Don't ignore her. Be respectful, cordial. Give her feedback if she starts talking to u. But don't be the initiator. Don't be so conversational and buddy buddy. U know she can turn on u at any time. In regards to her snapping on u when u told her the other day that she should be resting, in the future don't offer her any advice unless she asks u for it.

Tuesday November 5, 2013, 3:11pm

Mia: Did she say something about me?

Me: No. Just thinking about this from what you said yesterday.

Mia: And I learned my lesson about offering unsolicited advice to her. I'm not even gonna offer it if she asks for it because it just goes in one ear and out the other anyway

Me: Right

Wednesday November 13, 2013, 9:21am

Mia: Fuck me. Your mother is off today.

Me: Tomorrow may be her regular day off too.

Mia: No. Luckily it isn't.

Wednesday November 13, 2013, 10:57am

Me: Is she working this weekend?

Mia: No☹

Me: Drat!

Thursday November 21, 2013, 12:11pm

Me: Just my luck this morning. Go down to make breakfast at about 11:40 and she is in the kitchen watching mass and chanting right along with it. I had just a t shirt on and I went outside to close the gate. As I'm opening the door she breaks out of her chanting and shouts out, "don't go outside like that baby, it's cold!" I ignored her and went outside. When I came back in I wanted to say "if u don't stop babying me I'm gonna smack the shit out of u." There's no talking to her about it so what else can I do? The other day she said something to u in Creole to the effect that she wasn't comfortable seeing me carrying a lot of stuff upstairs. C'mon! I'm an adult, I'm a grown man.

Mia: Bill, I know mom can be overbearing and controlling at times. I'm not taking sides here, because lord knows I'm always on her shit list, but pick your battles. Sometimes you allow yourself to get a little too upset over little things like that

"Over little things like that," she says. I have listened to Mia complain about Mom and Pop so much and I've never dismissed her complaints as making a big deal about nothing. I was very angry when I read that text.

Mia: I have a chronic and debilitating illness too, and she couldn't care less about coddling me

Not sure why Mia needs Mom coddling her. Mia's a grown woman. I've come to realize that this is where Mia and I differ significantly. I don't want people coddling me when I'm sick or having problems, especially not my mother. I want to be left alone and deal with things myself. Mia doesn't seem to have the same independent mindset that I have. She would rather have someone to lean on—even if it's her mother who she has a love-hate relationship with—instead of working through difficulties on her own.

Me: U don't understand. I guess I would have to have a brother to understand where I'm coming from. And you've got to let go of this thing where u seem to be jealous of how she deals with me compared to u. If there is a difference, I didn't ask for it. I don't even like her. U vent to me about her like crazy about how she doesn't leave u alone, then u bitch that she's been acting aloof towards u. Where do u stand with her? Seems like she has become your best friend or at least a good one. Don't u see that?

Mia: Trust me, she is far from my best friend and there is no balance with her. I don't want her up my ass all the time, but I don't like being ignored. And she's only up my ass when she's kissing it because she needs something. It's not a jealousy, it just is. She favors you. She handles you with kid gloves and she lights into me for any piece of crap

That text was a lot of bullshit and nonsense.

Me: Well I wish I could vent to u about her without feeling like u r apologizing for her. Sorry u feel that way about the special treatment thing. Again, I don't want it. I want her off my dick.

Mia: We'll talk later. I think some sentiments are hard to express via text

I don't remember us having the talk she wanted to have, but I wasn't looking for it anyway. I already said my piece.

Sunday November 24, 2013, 12:58pm

Mia: Hey where u at?

Mia: Won't tell the elders.

Me: Amazing. You came to my mind seconds before your text. Nothing fun, I'm at dialysis. My dialysis schedule this week is Sunday Tuesday Friday. They re-worked everybody's schedule so the workers can get Thanksgiving off.

Mia: Oh ok. Yeah that makes sense. Well see ya later. It's a bitch out there.

It was one of those raw windy days with snow showers.

Me: Yes it is. I've gotta watch football on a little standard def TV. I'm pissed. Sunday in the fall is sacred. Unfortunately I'm probably gonna have this Sunday schedule again when Christmas and New Years comes around.

Tuesday November 26, 2013, 11:46am

Me: By any chance have u talked to your mother in the last hour or so?

Mia: No why?

Me: She's gonna be staying home today and tomorrow. She saw the doctor this morning about an eye infection. She's gotta apply a compress and take drops 5 times a day. She's not comfortable doing that at work.

Mia: Thanks for the heads up. Don't you have dialysis today?

Me: Yes I'm there now.

Mia: Ok

Mia: Is it snowing out?

Me: It wasn't when I got here at 11am. Can't tell now. Don't have access to a window.

Mia: Oh ok. My office is in the basement and there are no windows down here. I just heard someone say it was snowing

Me: It's still well above freezing. 39 degrees to be exact. Anything falling now is just wet non accumulating stuff.

Mia: Ok. Thanks for the weather update.

Monday December 2, 2013, 1:31pm

Mia: Let me tell you what your father did to me last night

Mia: He has the nerve to come knocking on my door asking, "can you and your brother pay $92?" I said no of course

Mia: I didn't even ask what it was for because I assumed it was the water bill. I was right, because when I was leaving this morning, I saw a check that he wrote for the water bill in the exact amount that he was asking for

Mia: He's pulled that stunt twice already after I specifically told both of them, beyond what I contribute on a monthly basis, don't approach me with shit else

Mia: I was livid

Me: Fuck um

Mia: If shit is getting that tight, file for bankruptcy or go into foreclosure, do something other than lying on your back expecting the sky to suddenly open up and start raining money or expecting me to dig deeper into my pockets

Our father is retired and relies on social security income. Our mother assigned him with the responsibility of paying the water bill, yet he's always trying to pass off the responsibility to us when Mia already contributes $400 a month to help with the mortgage and I pay $200 a month for the cable bill while being on a fixed income. The water bill is only due every three months for about $100 each time. Not sure why it's so hard for him to set aside about $35 a month so he'll have the money when the water payment is due.

Sunday December 22, 2013, 12:46am

Me: Would I rather have your health issues or keep mine? Tough question.

Mia: It's a catch 22. I certainly wouldn't wish ulcerative colitis on u or anyone. To live your life at the whim of your stomach is horrible. I've shit on myself more times than you care to know, most recently at work. I can't remember the last time I slept through a night because I wasn't going to the bathroom all night. I never have any energy because I'm so anemic from shitting blood all the time. Not saying I'm worse off than you, but both situations suck

Me: What I'd wanna do if I won some 500 mil lottery is give u half and we'd travel all over the world looking for cures for our diseases.

Mia: That would be awesome. Know that if I came into a huge sum of money, you would def be taken care of

Me: I know. Luv ya.

Mia: Right back at ya!

Tuesday December 24, 2013, 11:32am

Me: Did ya hear that mother is gonna b off next Monday Tuesday and Wednesday?

Mia: Nah. When did she tell you?

Me: Today

Mia: How sneaky. And she had the nerve to ask me why I didn't tell her I was on vacation. What a sneak.

Mia: Great, I get to spend the last three days of my vacation with her. That's gonna suck.

Mia: Anyway, good lookin out

Me: Yeah. Hate this time of year with all the adjusted schedules on TV and otherwise. Looking forward to The Honeymooners marathon though.

Mia: Absolutely

Me: U got a couple of the workers here at my dialysis clinic walking around with reindeer antlers on, including this Asian chick who's built like a small male sumo wrestler. Have you ever seen a fat reindeer?

Mia: Lol!!! You should take a pic

Me: I'll try to sneak one. Actually it was on Sunday that I saw the fat chick with the antlers. Haven't seen her yet today though. I'll keep a lookout.

Mia: Ok

Mia: Do you mind making a pit stop on your way home?

Me: What do u need?

Mia: I was craving some McDonald's if you happened to have the money and I would pay you back Thursday.

Me: What do u want?

Mia: 10 piece chicken nuggets (with BBQ sauce please), medium fries, a cheeseburger and a large vanilla shake

Me: Are u ordering for 2 days? Jeez. U know there are certain types of foods that'll b more likely to upset your bowels.

Mia: I could have added on two apple pies

Mia: Sometimes you just want comfort food even if it's not good for u. And thank you for the concern about my bowels

Me: I understand. I'll get the stuff if u really want it. Hope it's worth it.

I didn't really understand, but I was just being nice. Mia tells me frequently that she ends up doing a lot of emotional eating, which is a big reason why she's had weight problems over the years. I don't understand how people can be so obsessed with food, especially garbage food that's harmful to you. In the same way, I don't understand alcoholics and drug addicts either.

Mia: Many thanks. And yes, I do really want it.

Me: Ok

Me: This strict no salt diet of mine has led to me craving potato chips. Can't go there though cause the sodium and the potassium from the potatoes will raise my bp and add to the fluid in my body. And the fluid could go to my lungs and I won't b able to sleep and I'll be out of breath after taking a few steps. Maybe I might b able to do some low sodium corn chips, but I'm scared of even doing that. It's a sucky life. Before I got sick, I didn't eat potato chips much at all, but it's tough feeling restricted from doing that at least once in a while.

Mia: I know it is. I was watching an episode of Law & Order SVU last week about black market body parts. It especially focused on two patients who desperately needed kidney transplants. It hit home in more ways than you know

Mia: I thought of you the entire episode. At work, I sometimes have to schedule appointments for kidney donors. You don't know how much it breaks my heart. I hate that this is the hand that you've been dealt and how pop tried to say it was your fault. I can see why you're so pissed off at him. Only an insensitive jerk would pour salt on an already festering wound.

Me: Yeah. He's a jerk, and a dumbass. Btw, the water restriction thing sucks way more than the salt restriction thing.

Mia: I'm sure

Me: 7 months ago I bought a canister of sugar for myself (the yellow can on my fridge in my room), and it's just running out now. When I used to buy that same size canister for me and him, I had to buy another one every month

Mia: Wow.

Our father loves coffee. He must have at least two cups a day, and he puts gobs of sugar in it. It really boggles the mind as to how someone who takes in so much caffeine can fall asleep so easily.

I had a falling out with Mia on New Year's Eve. I went down to the kitchen at around 5pm to cook my dinner, and my sister and mother were already down there preparing a cake. They were listening to music on Mia's ipad, and it was turned up so loudly that it was literally making my ears hurt when I went into the kitchen. So I shouted towards Mia, "Would you please turn that down, it's hurting my ears!" The music was so loud that I felt compelled to shout so I knew I would be heard clearly. Mia took umbrage somehow with what I said or with the tone that she thought she perceived. So instead of turning the music down, she cops an attitude as she completely turned the music off.

An argument ensued, and our mother tried to be the moderator. I was trying to explain to Mia that I didn't want her to turn the music off, I just wanted it turned down because it was hurting my ears. I wanted her to turn it back on, but she refused. She said she didn't want to listen to it at a lower volume. She was just getting an attitude for no reason, and she refused to admit she had an attitude.

By the time I was done making my food, we finally reached an understanding. I got her to understand that I didn't have an attitude when I asked her to turn the music down, and I apologized if she perceived that I was mad. Mia finally admitted that she did have an attitude when she decided to turn the music off altogether, and she apologized. We had said some harsh things to each other in the heat of the moment, but all was forgiven.

Friday January 3, 2014, 12:58pm

It's just the early going of one of the snowiest winters in the Northeast I can ever remember.

Me: Made it to dialysis ok. They told me to be here at 1pm, but they're not ready yet so I've gotta sit in the waiting room. So what happened with mom?

Mia: She stayed at work last night. She didn't work though. She just slept somewhere. She's still there. She's working a double shift. She won't be home until tonight.

Mia: Glad you made it ok. How are the roads?

73

Me: Well as expected, the streets around our house are a mess. Once I was able to get through that and get on the highway, I had no problem.

Me: The weather forecast technology is so advanced now. They're rarely wrong anymore.

Mia: I know. Scary.

Me: Remember as a kid when u were expecting a snow day, and you would get up at 6am and look out the window to find that the roads were completely black? Hated that.

Monday January 6, 2014, 2:05pm

Mia: Hey Bill. Do you think you can pick me up from work @ 5 today? My engine light was blinking this morning and the engine was vibrating and smelled like smoke. I'm afraid to drive it home. I was going to drop it off at Firestone so they can work on it tomorrow.

I didn't text Mia back because I was in a lot of distress at my dialysis session. My treatment time was cut a half hour short because my blood pressure got very high and I think I was having seizures. My arms kept moving uncontrollably. I think the seizing was a reaction to a blood pressure medication they gave me. My treatment was suspended at around 2:30pm, and I remained sitting in my chair seizing for over two hours. I was in a haze, and my arms wouldn't stop moving. I thought I was dying. I was waiting for my heart to stop. Finally at around 5pm, the involuntary movements had ceased for a while and I decided that I had to try and get up and get ready to drive home. If I remained at the clinic any longer, I was risking that the clinic was going to have me hospitalized. I wanted nothing to do with going to the hospital, so it was time for me to get up and get out.

I was able to move around normally and drive home. I noticed Mia's text when I got to my car, and I called her to make sure she was okay with her car situation. I apologized for not getting back to her earlier. I didn't go into details. All I said was that I had a really tough dialysis session and I wasn't allowed to go home until my blood pressure went down to a normal range.

Tuesday January 21, 2014, 12:05pm

Mia: Did your package come yet?

Me: Yes

Mia: Good. How bad is it out there?

Me: They said the heaviest snowfall will be during the evening rush. You may want to come home early while the roads are decent and while there is still not too much snow in the backyard. Only about 2 inches so far.

Mia: I want to leave early but we don't have that option here. I'm hoping they will let us leave.

Me: Snowfall looks like it's in a slacking off period right now.

Tuesday January 21, 2014, 3:26pm

Mia: What's doing outside now? Doesn't look like they're letting us go home early.

Me: Snowfall has started again, and pretty strong for past hour.

Mia: They just told us they're letting us go at 4:30, which is only a half hour earlier than normal, but it's better than nothing. At least it'll still be light out.

Me: Drive carefully. The streets in our neighborhood are a mess.

Mia: Greeeaaaat

Wednesday January 22, 2014, 10:45am

Mia: I see you shoveled last night. I owe you a debt of gratitude.

Me: Thanks. Was out there for 2 hours. I really wasn't cold despite -10 degree windchill. At one point I had a mucus stream hanging from my nose. The temperature was so low that the mucus stream froze!

I did so much shoveling in the winter of 2014. In the previous winter when we had our first significant snowfall, I was only a few weeks removed from a brain hemorrhage surgery so Mom refused to let me shovel even though I felt fine. Anytime it snowed that winter, she told my then 79 year old father to shovel immediately before I could get to it. From the point of the very first major snowfall of 2014, I made it clear that I was doing the shoveling no matter how fragile she thought I was.

Wednesday January 22, 2014, 1:02pm

Mia: Well thank you for enduring the cold and mucus icicles to dig us out. If you hadn't, I don't think I would have been able to dig out and get to work on time. Did the dialysis clinic open late?

Me: They opened at 10, normally they open at 5am. My treatment time was scheduled for 1pm. I'm in my car outside the clinic right now cause when I went inside, they told me my time was moved to 1:30.

Mia: So glad ya mammy is finally going back to work today. If I knew how to do a cartwheel, I would do one right now.

Mia: Silence shall once again prevail, well, except for Bigfoot.

Bigfoot is in reference to our father and the manner in which he traverses the stairs. He traverses the stairs a lot, and he has very heavy footsteps.

Me: You know I'm an atheist, but...Amen!

Mia: Lol

Me: Heard that The Wanted is breaking up.

Mia: Whaaaat?!

Mia: I didn't think they were still in the limelight.

Mia: Justin Bieber's on a downward spiral trying to build a reputation as a badass.

Me: Ever since he changed from floppy hair over forehead to the hair pulled back look, it's like he's trying to reincarnate James Dean.

Mia: Lol. To me it's more like he's emulating Vanilla Ice.

Me: Yeah I can see that. Bieber has been making so much negative news that even mom knows who he is now.

Mia: Sad

Mia: And we know how mom loves to judge.

Me: Nothing like making news 4 scandalous behavior to get mom to know a celebrity, like Tiger Woods 4 example.

Mia: And Lady Gaga

Don't remember what Lady Gaga did that was scandalous, but ok.

Mia: And Rihanna (that's pop's favorite)

Mia: And most recently, Miley Cyrus

Me: Can't say Chris Christie is on that list. That's mom's guy so she's very familiar with him already. Bill Maher refers to him as Governor Chrispy Cream.

Mia: Lol

I mentioned Chris Christie because he was all over the news at the time because of the George Washington Bridge lane closure scandal. He had to be the one behind the lane closures, but it just cannot be proven. In my mother's eyes however, he can do no wrong. He had a long press conference where he repeatedly indicated that he had nothing to do with the lane closures, and of course Mom blindly believed him.

Mia: He lost some weight though. Haven't seen him recently, don't know if he's keeping it off

Hard to comprehend how Mia hadn't seen Governor Christie lately, given that he was all over the news at this time because of the lane closure scandal. Oh yeah, she rarely watches the news.

Me: Somehow he's still huge, yet if u look at the tape of him from last year, you can see he's noticeably smaller.

Mia: A car just crashed into a Pathmark in Irvington.

Mia: What's up with cars crashing into buildings lately?

Me: Maybe some roads still have snow on them.

Friday January 24, 2014, 4:59pm

Me: Unbelievable. Mom just came home sick. She said she's got a fever.

Monday January 27, 2014, 4:04pm

Me: She's not going tomorrow. She saw her doctor today and got a doctor's note. For the moment, she's going back to work on Wednesday.

Mia: Damn. Ok

Tuesday January 28, 2014, 10:36am

Mia: Who's playing in the SB this Sunday?

Tuesday January 28, 2014, 12:58pm

Me: Denver Broncos vs Seattle Seahawks. Why?

Mia: Oh nothing. One of my coworkers is going to a tailgate party and she said she didn't even know who was playing.

Me: Funny. It's the power of Super Bowl Sunday. People just welcome the opportunity for a party even if they don't know what the occasion is about. They wanna get a piece of the hoopla.

Mia: Yup

Mia: And they'll all be calling out on Monday

Mia: It's the biggest call out day of the year

Me: Yeah, that's why it's been talked about for years that the football season should start 2 weeks later so the SB would b pushed to the Sunday right before President's Day.

Mia: That's a great idea

Mia: However, President's Day is not a holiday for everyone

Me: Mom seems pretty good today. She's doing more moving around. Looks like she's gonna cook. A Wednesday return to work for her looks promising.

Mia: Beautiful!!! Still not holding my breath though. Too many fake outs

Tuesday January 28, 2014, 4:52pm

Mia: So you said mom was cooking something?

Me: Yes. Fish and cornmeal with greens mixed in.

Wednesday January 29, 2014, 9:43am

Mia: So ya mammy should be going off to work today?

Wednesday January 29, 2014, 11:09am

Me: I asked her at about 9:45 this morning if she was ready to go back to work. She said she was. Haven't heard her sneeze in a while and she's been moving around like normal. Think it's for real this time.

Wednesday January 29, 2014, 1:29pm

Mia: Ok. In the event that it isn't, please text me

Me: Sure will.

Wednesday January 29, 2014, 4:01pm

Me: Just got home and she's not here.

Mia: Yessssss!

Wednesday February 12, 2014, 11:19am

Me: Was stuck behind a driver this morning who fell asleep, literally. Was honking horn for at least 2 minutes b4 he finally woke up and moved. This ever happen to u?

Mia: Sometimes I do get stuck behind people who don't move right away when the light turns green and I wonder if they're asleep. That's scary that that person is on the road driving. You sure it wasn't Pop?

Me: Yeah, if anybody could sleep through 2 minutes of honking, it would b him.

Me: Doesn't sound like the gay football player that's trying to make the NFL has support from his parents. While his father said he loves his son and hopes he makes the NFL, he also said that he's an old school, men should be with women, type of guy. He said he doesn't want grand kids raised in a homosexual environment. That's a shame.

Mia: Yes that sucks.

The player I was referring to was Michael Sam, a University of Missouri grad who ended up getting selected in the 2014 NFL draft towards the end of the final round by the St. Louis Rams. Whether he'll make the final roster when the season starts in September remains to be seen.

Monday February 17, 2014, 10:59am

Me: Did u bring the trash inside this morning when it was still full?

Mia: Yes because since it's a holiday and I saw that it hadn't been picked up yet, I didn't think they were coming and the trash can was in the driveway blocking my path

Me: My bad, forgot about President's Day. Although I'm not sure if President's Day is one of the garbage pick-up holidays. BTW, mom's got a holiday today.

Mia: Thanks for the heads up. Good lookin out

Mia: I hear we're supposed to get more snow tomorrow. Any idea how much?

Me: I was just gonna ask u if more snow tomorrow was worse news than mom being home. There may be 2 inches on the ground by the time u leave for work tomorrow. During the day it will change to a rain/wet snow mix. High tomorrow is predicted to be 40 degrees.

Thursday February 20, 2014, 12:27pm

Mia: What's mom up to?

Me: She was out this morning. Came back around noon. Just went out again to see Chelsea. Looks like she's gonna cook fish.

Chelsea is a friend of Mom's who lives in our area.

Mia: Ok. Thanks. I just hoped she wasn't on another one of her cleaning frenzies that I was going to have to hear about when I got home

Me: Doesn't look like it.

Mia: Thank you

Friday February 21, 2014, 12:37pm

Mia: Yesterday I was so pissed when I got home and saw that mom had practically taken up half my parking spot in the yard. And then she's telling me that I could squeeze in when I could hear the side of my car scraping against the mound of snow that's covering the cellar doors. I didn't wanna scrape my car anymore so I asked her to move her car. Then she had the nerve to cop an attitude.

Mia: I mean it's enough of a nightmare trying to get in the driveway when I get home because of all the snow mounds on the ground, and she makes it harder for me cause she's practically in my space. Fucking narcissistic bitch

Me: So she ticks u off over the parking spot, then when u come inside she's talking your ear off as you're trying to go upstairs to your room

Mia: It never fails. Whenever I have the worst possible day at work and she happens to have the day off, she finds some way to further aggravate me. After I parked my car yesterday, she starts telling me all this long winded bullshit about her day with Chelsea and she's following me as I'm trying to walk away.

Me: I guess she didn't get to talk about Chelsea enough with u, so she was giving me the story after u went upstairs. I was thinking, "Does she even care that I'm not listening? Who's she talking to anyway?"

Mia: That's what I was thinking. I couldn't have acted anymore disinterested and she just kept fucking talking. I just wanted to scream: GET AWAY FROM ME!!!!!!!

Monday February 24, 2014, 12:14pm

Mia: How was Brunhilda this morning? Was she her usual bitchy self?

Me: Bitchy? Not really. Loud? Yes.

Mia: Well she was a biatch to the 10th power yesterday morning before she went to church of all places

I hadn't heard Mia refer to our mother as "Brunhilda" in a long time. I believe Brunhilda was an evil queen from the 6th century.

Tuesday February 25, 2014, 4:52pm

Mia: Did Brunhilda go to work?

Me: Yes

Wednesday February 26, 2014, 12:10pm

Mia: Do you have any idea how much snow we're supposed to get over the weekend? I'm hearing another big storm may be on the horizon

Me: Too early to tell.

Thursday February 27, 2014, 4:20pm

Mia: Do you still remember that drinking game you learned in college?

Me: Yeah, I'll show it to u later

Mia: Ok

That was a fun game back in the day when I could indulge in alcohol every weekend.

Sunday March 2, 2014, 12:58pm

Me: If u wanna watch the replay of Real Time with Bill Maher, it's coming up on Ch. 300 at 1:30.

Mia: Ok

I thought Mia might be interested in becoming more politically aware so I suggested she watch Real Time with Bill Maher on HBO. I doubt that she watched it though.

Tuesday March 4, 2014, 2:32pm

It's the day after Mia's 42nd birthday.

Me: Over the weekend I had a dream that we were expecting a major snow storm and it turned out to be nothing. Was it just a dream, or a premonition?

Mia: Or wishful thinking? Or a combination of all three

Mia: But damn if it ain't cold

Me: I'll take single digits everyday in exchange 4 no more snow!!

Mia: True that

I was wondering somewhat facetiously if my dream could've been a premonition, because in real life a major snowfall was predicted, and luckily the storm ended up completely missing our area.

Me: Mom was talking to me on Saturday about how she was making one of your favorite meals for your birthday and bought that little cake from ShopRite as well. Thought that dinky looking cake was a little lame. Would've been better if she baked a cake, or bought a real cake from a bakery. Thoughts?

Tuesday March 4, 2014, 3:44pm

Mia: Yeah, I thought it was rather lame myself, and I don't even like that kind of cake. I feel like I'm always going out of my way to spend money and time creating thoughtful things to do for her birthday or mother's day, but she never goes out of her way for me on my birthday. I don't even look forward to it anymore. It is no different from all the other 364 days in my year, with exception of being a year older

Me: I figured u felt that way. I remember a couple of years ago u were lamenting to me about how the parents have never fussed over u on your birthday.

Wednesday March 5, 2014, 11:04am

Me: Is it true that mom's retiring next month? She's going to be home now every single day? How are we surviving that? How are U surviving that?

Mia: It's not next month. It's May 1st. At least that's the date we decided on when I was filing for her retirement benefits online. So I don't know why she told you next month. How are we going to survive? I guess I'll be drinking a lot more. We gotta strategize

Me: Do u have numbers in terms of how much she makes a year versus how much the pension is going to give her?

Mia: No. But I got a glimpse of her W-2 for 2013. She made $45,621 and some change. That's twice what I made last year and then some. And she thinks I make more money than she does

Me: I thought I heard her say the pension was 30K? I hope I didn't hear that. If so, how's she making up a 15K budget deficit?

Mia: I'm sure most of what she earned last year was in overtime, but yeah you're right. That's why the damn house has to be relinquished SOON

Mia is right about the house having to be relinquished soon because the mortgage is such a big monthly expense, but thoughts about getting rid of the house make me squeamish because I'm left thinking "Where am I gonna live?" I would have thought that Mia would be thinking the same thing, but she has never seemed terribly concerned about the "Where is she gonna live?" part.

Me: The reverse mortgage thing, is she doing that?

Mia: We did try looking into that as an option. The owner of the house has to occupy the home during the loan period and there are a bunch of other stipulations. I did the research, but it was so long ago, I forgot all the particulars.

Mia: I think it may be worth revisiting though

Me: Would they let her work part time and still get her full pension?

Mia: I believe so. I think you're allowed to work a max of 20 hrs

Mia: Because early on in pop's retirement, he worked for K&G part time. Plus he had his newspaper delivery gig.

Mia: More and more retired people are working part time these days

Me: She's gonna have to do that then. If that 30K number is what the pension is, then 15K is a huge deficit.

Mia: The pension she's referring to is from her job. That is money that she put towards her retirement that her employer has matched. It is not 30K per year. It is not what she will receive from Social Security. We don't know what that amount is going to be yet

Mia: That's what happens when you don't adequately plan for your retirement

Me: Whatever the combination of pension and SS is, if it's not enough she'll have to work part time to make up the deficit.

Mia: Well you can tell her that

Mia: Plus, it's also contingent on what her living expenses will be once there's no mortgage and her and pop are in Florida.

And if or when those two things happen Mia, where are you and me going to go?

Me: Well until then, she'll have to work part time if she doesn't get enough benefits.

Thursday March 6, 2014, 11:21am

Mia: Hey Bill. Can you check out how much Rosetta Stone costs for me?

Me: It's a lot. $324

Mia: Damn. That's ridiculous. Ok thanks

Me: I talked to mom about her impending retirement. Apparently she's only got $659 a month coming for the pension. That's only $7908 a year. I mentioned it 3 times that she's gonna have to work part time if she doesn't get enough from SS. Of course she was resistant to that idea and starts bemoaning about her bad knees. So I kept saying, "where's the money gonna come from then?" She replied with, "I don't know." Anyway, I had to put the working part time thing out there. I also mentioned that she should apply for food stamps, which she agreed with. Gotta make sure these religious freaks are in touch with reality. She might think if she prays hard enough that the money will fall from the sky, or she might think that we're going to subsidize her retirement.

Mia: That's exactly what she's thinking

Tuesday March 11, 2014, 11:46am

Me: Sure wish mom would wear that tooth piece at home. Yeesh!

Mom has two front teeth missing from her top row. She wears a tooth piece when she goes out, but doesn't wear it enough when she's home. That gap is not a pretty sight.

Tuesday March 11, 2014, 1:15pm

Mia: I started cracking up laughing after I read your text. My eyes started to tear up

Tuesday March 11, 2014, 3:50pm

Mia: It feels like summer...almost

Me: Roller coaster weather over next 10 days. 65 today. Normal high is about 49. Next 9 days: 55, 26, 46, 50, 40, 36, 39, 45, 48. Thankfully there's no snow in sight.

Friday March 14, 2014, 4:54pm

Me: She's home.

Mia: Word? Why?

Me: She's taking a personal day.

Mia: What is she doing right now?

Me: She's right in front of me in the kitchen.

Friday March 21, 2014, 5:28pm

Mia: Is she home?

Me: No

Mia: Thank fuck!

Monday March 24, 2014, 3:39pm

Mia: Did mom cook your chicken?

Me: Nope

Mia: Ouch

I eat the same thing for dinner everyday—chicken drumsticks, macaroni elbows and string beans. I cook a fresh batch of macaroni and string beans everyday, but because the chicken is much more of a time consuming process to cook, I'll only cook the drumsticks on Mondays and Fridays. I'll leave the leftovers in the refrigerator for the interim days until the drumsticks run out and I have to cook another batch. It can be tough cooking on Mondays and Fridays because on those days I'm just coming home from dialysis and sometimes I don't feel well.

Before I leave to go to dialysis, I'll take the chicken packages out of the freezer so they'll thaw out by the time I get back home. This is where my mother comes into play. I learned that she has a regularly scheduled day off every other Monday. I never ask her to cook my chicken on those days off, but usually if she sees that I left chicken out to defrost, she'll cook it by the time I get home. However, it seems like on the days when I feel the worst coming home from a dialysis session, it just so happens that those are the days when Mom doesn't cook my chicken even though she had the day off. Then I have to tough it out and cook it myself.

Tuesday March 25, 2014, 3:07pm

Me: You know she's off til Monday right?

Mia: No. I didn't know that. Why, she told you? Because she doesn't tell me shit. It's like she does it on purpose. I'm pissed now.

Me: She's nonchalant about this stuff. I was just washing my dish this morning and she's there and decides to share the news.

Mia: Anyway, as long as she leaves me alone. Lately I don't even care. I'm just numb.

Mia: Anyway, good lookin out

Me: Always

Mia: So what has she been doing all day?

Me: She's cooking. Looks like she's doing her usual "can't stay downstairs while she's cooking" routine. She was just annoying me a few minutes ago watching her religion channel and singing the hymns as she was moving around

Mia: Greaaaaat

Mom does not do a lot of babysitting of her cooking food. She'll start something cooking, put the cover on the pot and then go upstairs for several minutes. She'll end up periodically going back and forth up and down the stairs to check on the food. Sometimes she forgets to check on stuff too. She has set off a number of smoke alarms over the years, and she'll tend to leave the stove top a mess because sometimes things boil over when she's not there. Nevertheless, Mom is a good cook, but at times she's a negligent one.

Wednesday March 26, 2014, 3:58pm

Mia: Let me tell you what your mammy did this morning

Me: Let me have it.

Mia: Usually she's up at the butt crack of dawn praying in her room and watching that friggin Catholic channel. This morning when I was leaving for work at around 7:35, not only was she already up, she was also downstairs in the kitchen praying while watching that damn channel (which was turned up loud as usual). I'm like really. What the fuck. Like I really need this on my way out the door. So I drop my stuff in the living room because I had to go to the bathroom. I wasn't using the downstairs bathroom while she was downstairs, so I go use the upstairs one. I come back downstairs like 10 minutes later. I go to the living room to put my boots on and gather my stuff. Then of course she's gotta appear in the doorway and start staring at me asking if I'm ok. It's like really? I was thinking, "I'm just trying to get out of here, just get away from me. I don't care if you're doing your shit, just stay out of my way." I was fuming

Me: Wow. You might have to get used to seeing her being up and about when you're leaving for work cause she's got all these off days coming.

Mia: Yeah. Fuck me

Mia: She's not going anywhere, so why does she have to be up at the ass crack of dawn and all up in my way and my business?

Me: Old people are just weird like that. An illustration of why parents and kids can't live in the same house after they reach a certain age.

Mia: Amen

Mia: Unfortunately, they don't see it that way

It was not unusual in my parents' homeland for grown up kids to live with their parents until they got married.

Friday March 28, 2014, 6:26pm

Me: So fuckin loud! Couldn't get upstairs fast enough.

Mia: I could hear her from here

I was cooking downstairs in the kitchen while my mother was downstairs on the phone. I could not finish and get up to my room fast enough to get away from that obnoxiously loud voice. Mia could clearly hear her from upstairs in her room, and that's even with her door closed.

Monday March 31, 2014, 1:18pm

Mia: I have a feeling mom is not going back to work today. She has a cold now. She was coughing and blowing her nose this morning. Let me know.

Me: Ok

87

Monday March 31, 2014, 4:00pm

Me: She went to work.

Mia: Cool. She may come back. She's done that before.

Me: Relax. Think positively.

Mia: Trying to. It's like getting bitten by a dog, then after that you're terrified of dogs

Mia can get so annoyed when she comes home from work to find that our mother has taken a surprise day off. One day I was in the kitchen when Mia came home after seeing our mother's car in the yard. Mia was so angry that it was scary. She was slamming her bags down, cursing and slamming doors. She was muttering, "I can't get a fuckin break!" It was really an over the top display. I was tempted to say to her, "Jeez, all that?" But she was scaring me, so I just let her vent and didn't say a word.

Tuesday April 1, 2014, 3:07pm

Mia: Did she go to work?

Me: Yes

Thursday April 3, 2014, 3:50pm

Mia: Did mom cook anything by any chance?

Me: I smell something cooking right now.

Mia: Word?

Sunday April 6, 2014, 5:50pm

Mia: R u gonna DVR Wrestlemania?

Me: It's too long. Can't.

Sunday April 6, 2014, 8:09pm

Me: The Shield match is on now.

At this point I had recently learned that Mia was becoming a WWE wrestling fan again—we used to watch wrestling together way back when we were kids in the 80s. So I ordered

Wrestlemania XXX and invited her to my room to watch it. It was a great show, but it's 4 hours long so I figured I would call Mia over when her favorite tag team—The Shield—was in action. I was surprised when Mia decided to stick around after The Shield match and ended up watching the last 2 and a half hours of the show with me.

Monday April 7, 2014, 8:17pm

Mia: You watching WWE?

Me: I'm watching til 9ish, then I gotta watch a game. How many chances does Triple H get to shut down Daniel Bryan? Jeez.

WWE has a weekly Monday night show called Monday Night Raw, and it can be a pretty wild 3 hour broadcast. Since Wrestlemania XXX, Mia has made a habit of watching Raw with me— she'll be watching in her room and I'll be watching in my room—and sometimes we'll text each other about what we're watching.

Monday April 7, 2014, 11:09pm

Mia: And the Shield just delivered their own brand of justice!

Me: After the game, I'm gonna watch the rest of the show.

Mia: Oops. Ok, sorry for the spoiler.

Mia was so excited about the end of the show that she forgot I was watching a game and was going to watch the rest of Raw via DVR.

Wednesday April 9, 2014, 12:15pm

I was at dialysis and was watching the 12pm news.

Me: The Ultimate Warrior, who we just saw this past weekend when he was inducted into the WWE Hall of Fame, collapsed and died yesterday while walking to his car! He was just 54.

Mia: What!!!!?

Me: Unbelievable. It's a tough business. These guys abuse their bodies with steroids and pain killers for years and years. So many of them die young. Maybe the WWE knew he was sick and wanted to celebrate him while he was still around to appreciate it. So sad.

The Ultimate Warrior was one of our favorite wrestlers when we were kids. He was a big fan favorite.

Mia: I could tell when The Ultimate Warrior was giving his induction speech that he seemed a little off. He looked like he was ready to collapse then. He was very sweaty and he kept stopping during his speech like he was short of breath.

Me: Another one bites the dust. Awful. Did u hear the story from around 2007 about the wrestler Chris Benoit?

Mia: Vaguely rings a bell

Me: He was a prominent and popular WWE wrestler. All the drug abuse warped his brain so bad that he killed his wife and kid before killing himself. At first it was just a sad story of a great wrestler and his family being found dead in their home. The WWE honored him at first. Then they learned what really happened, and I don't think Benoit's name has been mentioned on the air since.

Mia: So friggin sad. I'm still in shock

Me: I was fairly comfortable on the dialysis chair today until I heard that news of the Warrior's death. Makes me think too much.

There have been so many wrestlers over the years who have not lived very long past their 50th birthdays. The Ultimate Warrior's untimely death was another reminder of how much of a physical toll the business takes on these guys. It made me question whether I should even continue watching wrestling, but I just had to remind myself that these wrestlers know what they're getting into when they sign up. They are willing to accept the good and the bad.

Mia: Life is just way too fleeting at times. Talk about here today and gone tomorrow

Me: You know the top wrestlers probably make millions a year, but they don't really have healthcare from the company. And there's pressure on them to continue to perform even with injuries, which means a lot of pain killers. They know if they don't perform for a while, they can lose their spot in the pecking order. And I don't think they get paid if they're too hurt to perform.

Mia: Something has to change

Me: Absolutely. They make money off these guys for years and years, but if you can't perform anymore, you kind of get tossed aside.

Mia: They're like racehorses

Me: Yup. Now these guys know what they're getting into when they sign up to do this. They're not employees of WWE. They're more like independent contractors.

Mia: So that's why no benefits, no unions. They're not protected under any corporate policies or contracts. I hope they all have good lawyers

Me: Yup. I don't think lawyers can do much though if they signed up as independent contractors.

Mia: Guess you're right

Me: Check out this conspiracy theory I just heard on TMZ. The Undertaker was supposed to beat Brock Lesner at Wrestlemania, but it was changed mid match to make Lesner win cause apparently Undertaker suffered a real concussion during the match so they cut the match short and changed the ending so Taker could get rushed to the hospital.

Mia: What the? But that's just a theory

Mia: But very plausible

Me: I believe it's a true story though that he was hospitalized after the match for some reason.

Mia: He didn't look right after the match. It did take him a while to get back on his feet and reorient himself. I knew none of that was acting

Mia: And we haven't seen him since Wrestlemania

Me: This could be the end of the Undertaker's career. He is like 50 years old. Over the past 5 yrs or so, the trend has been that u don't see him after Wrestlemania till a couple of months before the next Wrestlemania when he accepts another challenge from someone wanting to break his streak. With no more streak to defend, this may b it for him.

Mia: Heartbreaking

Me: Yeah. He should have got to go out undefeated at Wrestlemania.

Mia: Absolutely

Monday April 14, 2014, 8:06pm

The first Monday Night Raw after the Ultimate Warrior's death begins with a very touching tribute.

Mia: My heart is breaking right now

Me: Yeah, my eyes got watery.

Mia: Mine too

Mia: Listening to the bell tolling was just a chilling moment

Me: How bout the speech The Ultimate Warrior gave just last week when he said, The Warrior would be running forever.

Mia: He will run forever...in the hearts of his fans. So in a way, what he said was a foreshadowing of future events. He is now immortalized in WWE history.

Me: Absolutely. Turned out to be haunting and prophetic words.

Mia: I'll say

Tuesday April 15, 2014, 2:33pm

Mia: Is mom home?

Me: No she went to work. And lucky you. You just missed people coming to look at the house.

Mia: Well no one told me and my room was a mess. Whatever. Now we're back to that bullshit again

Another futile attempt was made at trying to sell our house. It's a pretty big and pretty good looking house, other than the unfinished basement. Problem is the house is in a bad area, and the types of people that are willing to live in a bad area are lower income people. Unfortunately those are the people who have trouble getting home loans.

Wednesday April 16, 2014, 12:03pm

Me: Got an idea 4 a reality show, although I may be remembering something that's already been done. Engaged couples compete for a chance to win a super lavish, all expenses paid wedding. Could call it My Dream Wedding. Has this idea been done already?

Mia: I think it has

Me: Had a feeling. How bout married couples who hate each other compete to get their divorce paid for? That would be fun watching ppl who hate each other have to work together to get away from each other.

Mia: That would be fun to watch. Could call it Divorce Wars

Mia: But I think there is already a show on CNBC with that title. Not the same concept though

Me: Yeah we'd need another name. You know what would be interesting? How many of the winning couples would decide to stay together in the end cause working together naturally made them closer?

Mia: I was thinking exactly the same thing

Wednesday April 16, 2014, 3:58pm

Mia: Is she home?

Me: Nope

Mia: Thank u

Mia: I hate the months of April, May and June

Me: I know what you're getting at. The parents' birthdays and mothers/fathers days.

Mia: Yup. Fuckin hate it. But half of that is of no concern to you. You're so lucky.

Me: Yeah. Sorry. The situation makes me uncomfortable at times, but at least I get a nice perk. The first time I saw Pop after that blowup over the water back in February of 2013, I had to make a choice about whether I was going to acknowledge his presence when I came home and he was in the kitchen. Once I ignored him and just walked by silently, I accepted that that action was the end of our relationship (what little there was of one anyway). Can't go back. Won't go back.

Mia: I totally feel you

Me: You know what really made me lose it when I confronted him about that chicken leg? As I was expressing my indignation and irritation about how he couldn't deduce that the chicken leg was mine, he was trying to shout over me, saying 2 or 3 times "how much do you want for the chicken?" First off, it wasn't for sale. Secondly, his tone was dismissive. Like my ire wasn't taken seriously.

I was referring to an incident a couple of days earlier when I blew up on my father because he supposedly just "mistakenly" ate a chicken leg I left in the refrigerator. He said he didn't know it was mine. My point was that he should have figured it was mine because my routine for months had been to have one left over chicken leg in the refrigerator on Mondays from the batch I cook on Fridays.

Mia: I'm not trying to go into debt or spend money that I'm trying to save buying gifts for those two, especially when they don't make a real fuss over me...ever

Me: I feel ya.

Both of our parents' birthdays are in April, then Mother's Day and Father's Day are right around the corner. I get a pass on having to worry about half of those days because I have no relationship with my father. Mia doesn't get that pass, so she has to worry about all 4 days. There are actually 5 days that Mia should be thinking about during this time period. My birthday happens to fall in May, but I cannot remember the last time Mia did anything even remotely noteworthy for me. She barely acknowledges the day. I know she may be reluctant to acknowledge it because she knows that it's been a long time since I looked forward to a birthday. The last birthday I looked forward to was my 21st, and I've kind of been dreading birthdays since I turned 30. The years have just flown by and you're just getting closer and

93

closer to old age and death. Actually, forget about death. I'm much more scared of getting old and being old than of dying.

Despite everything I just said, I still appreciate being shown a little love on my birthday, but my sister has been negligent in doing that. Back on my year 2011 birthday when I was still living in my own place, I was waiting all day long for Mia to just give me a call. I went to bed that night rather bewildered because her call never came. Her call never came because she felt it was sufficient to wish me Happy Birthday, via email. I didn't happen to check my email until 3 days later. So for three days she had me thinking that she forgot or just blew off my birthday. Now I know that Mia has told me that she hates talking on the phone, but you've got to make an exception for your brother's birthday. C'mon now.

Wednesday April 16, 2014, 7:03pm

Me: Every now and then I gotta hear these little outbursts. It's like Family Feud is the best thing he's ever seen. It's not a big deal. Jeez

I could hear our father from his room having a good ol time watching Family Feud. He's obsessed with the Game Show Network. He'll be up past one in the morning every night watching that channel. Family Feud is probably his favorite.

Mia: He finds the most moronic things entertaining...like the Andy Griffith Show. I love my classic tv, but that show has never made sense to me

Me: He's getting more simple minded each passing day.

Thursday April 17, 2014, 4:39pm

Mia: Did mom cook anything?

Me: There's a small pot with some cornmeal in it. There's also some fish in a bowl that hasn't been prepared yet.

Friday April 18, 2014, 11:43am

Me: Would u b able to loan me 50 bucks? I'd pay u back in 2 weeks.

Mia: May I ask what for?

Me: I don't have enough money to buy food today and next Friday before I get my disability benefits on the following Friday (May 2nd)

I go to the market every Friday afternoon following dialysis.

Mia: Well how are you gonna buy food today if you don't have enough money and I don't get home till 5:30?

Me: I have enough for today, but not enough for today and next Friday combined.

Mia: Ok. However, as long as I get it back as agreed because this puts a big dent in my finances until I get paid again

Me: Thank u. And I'd never stiff u. I understand where you're coming from.

Mia: Ok. I probably won't be stopping by the bank today. When do you need it by?

Me: By next Thursday so I'll have it for next Friday.

Mia: Ok

I don't like asking people for money, but I felt okay asking Mia for 50 bucks here because she had recently told me that she had $3300 saved towards a new car. I didn't think it was a big deal for her to just take out $50 from that savings that would be put back in a couple of weeks anyway. However, it seemed like Mia had no intentions of touching that savings even if it was only for a relatively small short term loan.

I love how Mia said "Ok. However, as long as I get it back as agreed." As if I would stiff her. I would never break my word on paying her back, even though she has stiffed me on loans a number of times in the past.

Monday April 21, 2014, 1:00pm

Me: U would think mom would b knocked out in bed this morning after a double shift, but nooo. Her and the old man were both in my way in the kitchen. The guy likes to stand in front of the tv and near the fridge. I need to go in and out of the fridge, and he barely moves when I need to get in there. When mom was lecturing me last week about yelling at him over the chicken, she said she notices how I move on him without saying excuse me. To me, he should just see that he's in my way and step aside.

Mia: You're right, I agree

Me: Had to bite my tongue this morning to keep from saying to him, "get the fuck out of the way!"

Mia: Yeah you need to keep that in check

Mia: Why don't you try to make any effort to get out of there?

Me: U mean moving out?

Mia: No, changing rooms. Yes of course I mean moving out

95

Me: It's very hard to find a part time job that I could fit around my dialysis schedule. I would b allowed by the government to make up to 770 a month without getting my disability benefits reduced.

Mia's showing me here that she does not have an appreciation for how difficult my situation is. Even if I could find a job that would fit around my dialysis schedule, no one wants to hire someone who has not worked in 6 years. Plus I'm not sure I could pass a background check because I'm on probation. What I've been focusing on since the start of 2013 is writing with the hopes that I can get my story published and make it big.

She's wondering why I haven't tried to make any effort to get out of this house? Well I could say the same thing about her. She ended up back in the house because she lost a good job and had to settle for a much lower paying one. So all she has to do is look for a higher paying job, which shouldn't be hard for her to obtain because she has a wealth of experience and is great in interviews. Then before too long she would have the wherewithal to move out. Her solution to get out of the parents' house is pretty straightforward, yet she dares to question my motivation?

Monday April 21, 2014, 5:13pm

Mia: Did she cook your chicken?

Me: No. And get ready for a blow by blow account of what she was up to today.

Mia: After yesterday she's not talking to me, which is perfect

Monday April 21, 2014, 8:36pm

Mia: Are u watching Raw?

Me: Yep

Mia: What the fuck? How much fucking physical torture can they inflict on Daniel Bryan?

Me: That was tough to watch.

Mia: And then Stephanie McMahon is trying to make a feeble attempt to stop Kane and call him off when she unleashed him in the first place

Me: She's a witch.

Tuesday April 22, 2014, 11:04am

Mia: R u getting mom anything for her bday?

Me: I usually give her a "happy birthday" and a hug, then I spend money on her for Mother's Day

Mia: Gotcha

Tuesday April 22, 2014, 2:26pm

Mia: Please tell me she went to work.

Me: She just left

Mia: Gracias

Thursday April 24, 2014, 11:00am

Incidentally, this April 24th happens to be our parents' 45th anniversary. That sounds like it should be a big deal, but my sister and I have not acknowledged our parents' anniversary since we were kids. I guess it's a sad commentary. It just shows how little regard we have for those two. Plus particularly from my sister's perspective, it's very easy to take the anniversary day off in terms of gift giving or commemoration because she already has to deal with our father's birthday on the 17th and our mother's on the 23rd. Our parents haven't exactly been the most harmonious couple over the years anyway. Perhaps the only reason they aren't divorced is that it's too complicated and they can't afford to do it.

Me: Remember I need $50 to go to the market tomorrow. I'll pay u back next week.

Thursday April 24, 2014, 12:27pm

Mia: Already taken care of

Me: Thanks

Mia: Mmmmm hmmmm

I know I had told Mia the previous week that I needed the money by the following Thursday, but I didn't expect that she was actually going to keep me waiting until Thursday when I knew she already had the money when I had asked for it. I had to text her a reminder that I needed the money, and she replied with "Already taken care of." Well if you already had it, then why keep me waiting for 6 days? And when I said "Thanks," she responded with the "Mmmmm hmmmm." I know the tone of that Mmmmm hmmmm. That Mmmmm hmmmm is like her reminder to me that she didn't want to part with that money so I should really appreciate that she was doing me this huge favor.

So on Thursday April 24th she got home from work at around 5:30pm. I was in the kitchen when she got home, and I was waiting for her to hand me the money. I wasn't going to mention it again; I didn't want to seem pushy. So she grabs something out of the refrigerator and she goes upstairs with no mention of the $50. I was sweating it out a little here, because I was not going to be able to go to the market the next day without that money. She finally gave me the money about a half hour later.

Monday April 28, 2014, 3:28pm

Mia: Did she go to work?

Me: Yes

Mia: Awesome

Tuesday April 29, 2014, 4:20pm

Two days before our mother retires. Two days before she's home just about all day and everyday—being loud, being annoying.

Mia: These are our last two days of peace

Me: Hard to believe

Mia: Yesssss it is. I'm cringing.

Wednesday April 30, 2014, 1:02pm

Mia: Here's a blast from wrestling's past. Jesse the Body Ventura used to refer to this tag team as "Lucky Pierre and La Bamba." To which duo was he referring?

Me: Strike Force. What made u think of that?

Mia: I'm on my break now and I'm listening to Awesome 80s on my Aol radio app and that La Bamba song was just playing. That memory immediately came to mind.

Me: Did u see how the match between Randy Orton and Roman Reigns ended on Monday night?

Mia: Yessssss. Of course it ended up turning into a free-for-all. What a shock. But Roman and the boys sent Randy and the rest of Evolution running scared again, as they didn't have their band of 11 bastards as back up. I loved the nice dis by Rick Flair when he gave his laudatory words to the Shield instead of Evolution.

Mia: Love WWE. Never know what's going to happen, which as we learned, can be both good and bad. I think Daniel Bryan's wife should have slapped the shit out of Stephanie McMahon. Stephanie's apology was about as sincere as a politician's campaign speech.

Me: Absolutely. Nice comeback by the Shield. Evolution was taking it to them outside the ring. Didn't look good for a while. Then they went inside the ring and Rollins came out of nowhere from the top rope and kicked Triple H in the head. Turning point of the game.

Mia: Loooovvvvved it. Now I'm going to play devil's advocate here for a sec. I think Randy Orton is hot as hell, but it was nice to see him get a dose of whoop ass!

Mia: And I have to give credit where credit is due to Triple H. He can take his shirt off anytime. That man has a warrior's physique. I was drooling. He's not the most beautiful man, but damn what a beautiful body.

Me: You're funny. Hey I'm watching some fat fuck chef on The Talk showing the hosts his recipe 4 pancake lasagna. Really? Gross.

Wednesday April 30, 2014, 1:33pm

Me: FYI. Mom expressed her excitement to me this morning about her last day being today. I had the audacity to mention that she should ask her job if she can continue to work on a part time basis. She made it clear that that wasn't an option. She didn't get angry, but she made it clear. It's a job that's too physically taxing for her at her age and with her chronic knee problems. So I was like, "what type of work could u do that won't b too tough on u physically?" I mentioned I saw an ad about someone looking for a person to pick up their kids from school and babysit on weekends. She said she could handle something like that, although she wants to rest and allow her body to recuperate for a few weeks b4 looking into getting part time work. She expressed to me that ideally her kids should b taking care of her, but she knows that can't b in our case. I made sure I let her know that she was right about that. She reiterated hopes about selling the house so she can go to Florida. I was thinking, "that's great, but where does that leave me and Mia?" As I was leaving the kitchen, she uttered the bullshit about leaving things in god's hands. B4 I left her I said, "yeah but u've gotta have a plan though." She smiled and was like, "yeah yeah." Oh these religious freaks... If u wanna believe in god, u need to remember that god helps those who help themselves.

Mia: I'm just sick of her "my children should be taking care of me" bullshit

Me: That's why as soon as she finished saying that she knows that can't happen, I made sure to interject with a short and succinct "no."

Mia: She screwed herself by not planning for her retirement. Whose fucking fault is that? Not mine and not yours. You should never leave your financial future in anyone else's hands. That is why intelligent adults plan for their retirement years so that they don't have to be a financial burden on their kids.

Me: Absolutely. U've got a right to retire at 65, but she fails to appreciate that ppl like her with her economic circumstances can't afford to retire, at least not yet.

Mia: Exactly. Just wait. She'll see

Mia: It's unfair. She gave me one of the most fucked up childhoods that a parent could inflict on a child, which I'm still bearing emotional scars from, and then she expects that I'm supposed to take care of her?

Mia: She has no one to blame but herself, but knowing her, she will blame everyone and everything else for her failure.

Mia: And as far as selling the house, don't worry about me having a roof over my head. There's going to be a time in the not too distant future when I'm going to just leave one morning and not come back...just trying to work it out in my head

Me: Don't leave too rashly though. Have a good plan so u don't have to come back.

Mia has moved out of the house 4 times (in 1991, 2003, 2009 and 2010) and has ended up coming back 4 times.

Mia: You might have to help me brainstorm

Mia: I wish you hadn't sent me that first text. Now I'm upset.

Me: Sorry, but I felt u needed to know how this woman is thinking right now. The most practical route to go is 4 us to get a place together. I'm looking into UPS and Fedex jobs. I need a part time job that I can fit around dialysis. There are 5pm to 10pm shifts available that could b ideal.

Mia: I always knew that she had the idea of us taking care of her in her mind. I just tried to be oblivious to it. I'm not mad at you. Just pissed at the situation.

Me: I know. I feel ya about everything u've said.

Mia: We'll talk later. I'm getting a headache and I've lost my appetite.

So what's going to happen for the rest of 2014 and beyond as Mia and I face the new reality of having our mother home all the time? Will we figure out a way to leave the house before she and the old man drive us crazy? Will Mia and I be able to get our own places to live before the house gets sold? Will Mom ever accept that as long as the house isn't sold, she will have to work part time because the math is against her completely retiring? She's making about $13,000 less a year from the combination of her social security and her pension than she was making when she worked full time. The money to fill that $13,000 income gap is not coming down from the sky, no matter how hard she prays. If she doesn't get a job pretty soon, then perhaps the best case scenario is that we end up having to live with no electricity and no water. The worst case scenario would be the bank foreclosing on the house and kicking us all out.

If you're interested in a more detailed story of the life of Michael Jean DuBois, you can find my memoir on Amazon titled, The Story of Mr. Anti-Social. *Also be on the lookout on Amazon for part 2 of Texting Mia,* Texting Mia PTII.